OWN IT! 2

PROJECT BOOK

Simon Cupit

CAMBRIDGE
UNIVERSITY PRESS

Shaftesbury Road, Cambridge CB2 8EA, United Kingdom

One Liberty Plaza, 20th Floor, New York, NY 10006, USA

477 Williamstown Road, Port Melbourne, VIC 3207, Australia

314–321, 3rd Floor, Plot 3, Splendor Forum, Jasola District Centre, New Delhi – 110025, India

103 Penang Road, #05-06/07, Visioncrest Commercial, Singapore 238467

José Abascal, 56–1°, 28003 Madrid, Spain

Cambridge University Press & Assessment is a department of the University of Cambridge.

We share the University's mission to contribute to society through the pursuit of education, learning and research at the highest international levels of excellence.

www.cambridge.org
Information on this title: www.cambridge.org/9781108726641

First published 2020

20 19 18 17 16 15 14 13 12 11 10 9 8 7

Printed in Great Britain by Ashford Colour Press Ltd.

A catalogue record for this publication is available from the British Library

ISBN 978-1-108-72664-1 Own it! Project Book Level 2
ISBN 978-8-490-36882-4 Collaborate Project Book Level 2

Additional resources for this publication at www.cambridge.org/ownit/resources

CONTENTS

AN INTRODUCTION TO PROJECT WORK

Welcome back to school! Your students are waiting for new challenges. How are you going to help them develop their skills this year?

Your class has now experienced project work. Students have worked together in groups to produce and present their projects to the class. At the same time, they have used and developed their language skills to communicate. The projects in Level 2 are designed to help your students expand their learning possibilities and stay motivated.

This book will guide you on how to make the most of your projects, so your students can continue to work successfully both in and out of the classroom.

What is project work?

Imagine you and your class have just finished Unit 6 (Hidden danger). Your students have learned vocabulary for parts of the body and practised making suggestions to avoid accidents and injuries. How can you review and expand on this topic? In this case, your students make an information leaflet, with suggestions for how to stay safe.

As you know, this is project work: students taking ownership of their work and making decisions together. There is a final objective and a series of stages to follow, where groups can explore how to achieve their goals. The final aim is always a presentation stage. **> Presentation ideas p18** Your role is to help this happen. As a result, students learn by doing and share memorable experiences.

Throughout the project work process, students develop a number of **life skills**. They learn to:

Create new ideas

Question actively

Use social skills

Think critically

Work collaborativ

Create

BENEFITS AND ADVANTAGES OF PROJECT WORK

✓ Personal advantages

- encourages **creativity** by promoting **different ways of thinking**
- increases **motivation** through challenge
- develops **autonomy** and a **sense of responsibility**
- increases natural **curiosity**
- improves **self-knowledge** through **self-evaluation**
- improves **communication skills** through teamwork
- involves family and friends in the **learning process**
- improves **interpersonal** relationships
- develops **life skills**

✓ Academic advantages

- allows teachers to deal with **mixed-ability** classes
- motivates whole-team / cooperation / group work and promotes chances to **learn from one another**
- develops **planning** and **organisational skills**
- offers a '**flipped classroom**' approach
- **helps learning** through research and opportunities for deep thinking
- increases opportunities to **integrate cross-curricular** and **cultural topics**
- encourages **peer teaching** and **correction**
- enables students with **different learning styles** to help one another

✓ Language learning

- provides opportunities to **use language naturally**
- integrates all **four skills** (reading, writing, listening and speaking)
- allows for the use of **self- and peer-evaluation language**
- encourages research and **use of English out of the class**
- is learner-centred: students **learn language from one another**
- practises both **fluency** and **accuracy** through different types of presentations

Project work and the Cambridge Life Competencies Framework

How can we prepare our students to succeed in a changing world? We see the need to help students develop transferable skills, to work with people from around the globe, to think creatively, analyse sources critically and communicate their views effectively. However, how can we balance the development of these skills with the demands of the language curriculum?

Cambridge have developed the Cambridge Life Competencies Framework. This Framework reinforces project work, helping teachers recognise and assess the many transferable skills that project work develops, alongside language learning.

The Framework provides different levels of detail, from six Competencies to specific Can Do Statements. The Competencies are supported by three foundation layers.

Critical Thinking	Creative Thinking	Collaboration	Communication	Learning to Learn	Social Responsibilities

EMOTIONAL DEVELOPMENT AND WELLBEING	DIGITAL LITERACY	DISCIPLINE KNOWLEDGE

It then defines specific Core Areas. For example, here are the Core Areas for Collaboration :

Taking personal responsibility for own contribution to a group task.	Listening respectfully and responding constructively to others' contributions.	Managing the sharing of tasks in a project.	Working towards a resolution related to a task.

Then, there is a Can Do statement for each Core Area. These will differ depending on the age of the students.

Competency
Collaboration

↓

Core Area
Managing the sharing of tasks in a project

↓

Can Do Statements
- Follows the instructions for a task and alerts others when not following them.
- Explains reasons for suggestions and contributions.
- Takes responsibility for completing tasks as part of a larger project.

For more information, go to:
cambridge.org/elt

Level 2 Projects	Competency	Core Area	Can Do Statements
The culture project: a storyboard for an advert — Teacher's Resource Bank Unit 1	Creative Thinking	Creating new content from own ideas or other resources	*Communicates personal response to creative work from art, music or literature.*
	Learning to Learn	Reflecting on and evaluating own learning success	*Selects and uses a wide range of mind maps and other tools to organise thoughts; Identifies what needs to be revisited before identifying new learning goals.*
The history project: a museum display — Student's Book pp30–31	Collaboration	Listening respectfully and responding constructively to others' contributions	*Listens to / acknowledges different points of view respectfully; Evaluates contributions from other students with appropriate sensitivity.*
	Communication	Managing conversations	*Can use simple techniques to start, maintain and close conversations of various lengths; Uses appropriate strategies to develop a conversation (e.g. showing interest).*
The culture project: a comic strip — Teacher's Resource Bank Unit 3	Critical Thinking	Synthesising ideas and information	*Selects key points from diverse sources to create a new account.*
	Social Responsibilities	Taking active roles including leadership	*In group work, makes consultative decisions; Encourages others to participate and contribute in projects.*
The social studies project: a poster — Student's Book pp54–55	Social Responsibilities	Understanding personal responsibilities as part of a group and in society	*Understands various aspects of society (e.g. volunteering); Gets involved in collective action in the school (e.g. through volunteering).*
	Creative Thinking	Using newly created content to solve problems	*Employs new ideas and content in solving a task or activity; Makes an assignment original by adding new angles.*
The culture project: a poster — Teacher's Resource Bank Unit 5	Learning to Learn	Practical skills for participating in learning	*Participates sensibly and positively in learning activities in class; Understands essential grammatical terms and concepts.*
	Collaboration	Managing the sharing of tasks in a project	*Ensures that work is fairly divided among members in group activities; Offers to help others finish a task.*
The science project: an information leaflet — Student's Book pp78–79	Critical Thinking	Understanding and analysing links between ideas	*Compares points and arguments from different sources; Identifies the basic structure of an argument.*
	Communication	Managing conversations	*Uses appropriate language to negotiate meaning: to show understanding; to signal lack of understanding; to seek clarification.*
The culture project: a 3D room plan — Teacher's Resource Bank Unit 7	Critical Thinking	Evaluating ideas, arguments and options	*Examines possible solutions to a given problem and states how effective they are; Assesses strengths and weaknesses of possible solutions.*
	Collaboration	Working towards a resolution related to a task	*Is aware when others have divergent views and ideas for solving a problem or task; Is able to propose solutions that include other views and ideas to own.*
The design and technology project: a timeline — Student's Book pp102–103	Learning to Learn	Practical skills for participating in learning	*Uses metacognitive strategies (e.g. time management) to maximise learning; Takes effective notes in class and from homework reading.*
	Creative Thinking	Creating new content from own ideas or other resources	*Writes or tells an original story, given prompts or without prompts; Responds imaginatively to contemporary or historical events and ideas.*
The culture project: a webpage — Teacher's Resource Bank Unit 9	Communication	Managing conversations	*Uses appropriate language to negotiate meaning: to check own understanding; to check interlocutors' understanding; Invites contributions from interlocutors in a conversation.*
	Social Responsibilities	Understanding and describing own and others' cultures	*Makes informed comparisons between their own society and other societies; Understands the contributions of different cultures to their own lives.*

HOW TO USE THE *PROJECT* BOOK

See learning outcomes at a glance, as well as the skills students will develop and the resources and evaluation tools you may wish to use.

Manage student roles and responsibilities.

Monitor and check the skills that project work develops, mapped to the Cambridge Life Competencies Framework.

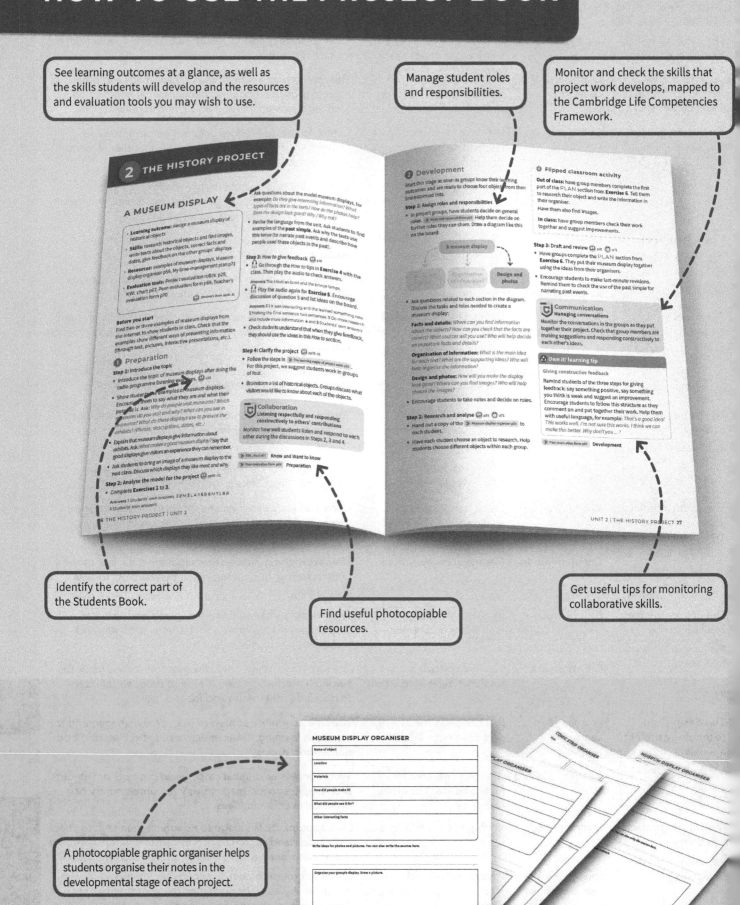

Identify the correct part of the Students Book.

Find useful photocopiable resources.

Get useful tips for monitoring collaborative skills.

A photocopiable graphic organiser helps students organise their notes in the developmental stage of each project.

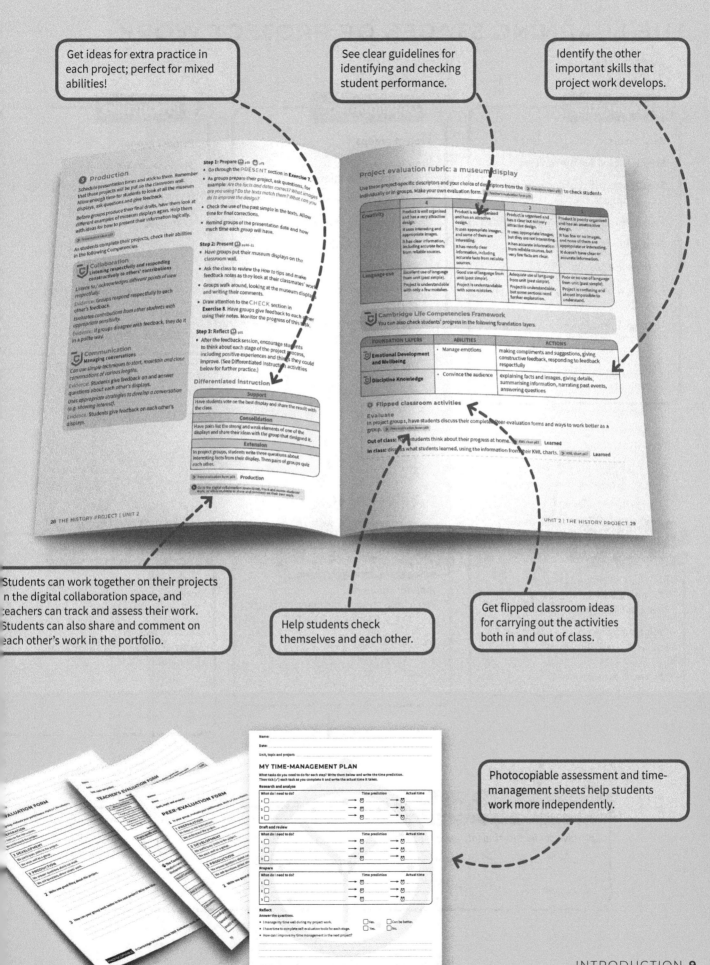

Get ideas for extra practice in each project; perfect for mixed abilities!

See clear guidelines for identifying and checking student performance.

Identify the other important skills that project work develops.

Students can work together on their projects in the digital collaboration space, and teachers can track and assess their work. Students can also share and comment on each other's work in the portfolio.

Help students check themselves and each other.

Get flipped classroom ideas for carrying out the activities both in and out of class.

Photocopiable assessment and time-management sheets help students work more independently.

THE LEARNING STAGES OF PROJECT WORK

1 Preparation

Facilitators

Step 1: Introduce the topic

Step 2: Analyse the model for the project

Step 3: Go through the *How to* tips

Step 4: Clarify the project

- Organise groups
- Review the learning outcomes and skills
- Brainstorm ideas
- Focus on key information
- Have groups make decisions about content

2 Development

Project groups

Step 1: Assign roles and responsibilities

Step 2: Research and **analyse**

Step 3: Draft and **review**

- Put together work
- Peer-correct
- Express opinions and make choices

3 Production

Project groups

Step 1: Prepare

- Decide how the project will look and who will speak
- Practise

Step 2: Present

- Take turns presenting
- Ask questions and give feedback

Step 3: Reflect

- Discuss all stages of the process

Pre-evaluation (self-evaluation)

Tools for students:
KWL chart, My learning diary, Peer-evaluation form

Tools for teachers:
Teacher's evaluation form

> Evaluation tools pp67–70

Formative evaluation (self-evaluation, peer-evaluation, observation)

Tools for students:
KWL chart, My learning diary, graphic organisers, Peer-evaluation form

Tools for teachers:
Teacher's evaluation form

> Evaluation tools pp67–70

Formative and summative evaluation

Tools for students:
KWL chart, My learning diary, Peer-evaluation form

Tools for teachers:
Teacher's evaluation form, Evaluation rubric

> Evaluation tools pp67–70

> Evaluation rubric p21

Reflection (you and students)

1 Have *student-to-student*, *student-to-teacher* and *teacher-to-student* discussions on evaluation grades.

2 Identify areas for improvement in future projects using the Evaluation tools.

> Evaluation p20

L1 IN PROJECT WORK

Many teachers believe that the only way for students to learn English effectively is by using it at all times in class. They feel that any time students spend using their own language is a missed opportunity.

Do you allow L1 use in your classroom? If you do, don't worry: there is little data to support the above idea (Kerr, 2016)[1]. In fact, there are occasions when allowing students to use L1 is positive. This is particularly true of project work.

We can use L1 in different steps of the project cycle. Take *Clarifying the project* as an example (Preparation stage, Step 4). If students fail to understand the project's objectives, they won't carry it out properly. Allowing L1 use is not a 'missed opportunity' here. It ensures a richer project experience.

Of course, this doesn't mean you should use students' own language *all* of the time. You have to consider factors like age, level, the complexity of the project and its outcomes. The question is not *if* you should use own language, but *when, how* and *how much*.

At Level 2, we suggest you allow own-language use for explaining or discussing things in more detail. However, students should be using more English in the development and presentation stages.

✓ Tips for L1 use

- Set rules for when students can use L1.
- Encourage groups to monitor their own-language use and think of ways to use more English.
- Allow students 'own-language moments' (Kerr, 2014: 26–29)[2], such as preparing for speaking activities. Remember that the students' goal is to produce English in the Production stage of project work.

OL = Own language, E = English, shows suggested language

THE LEARNING STAGES OF PROJECT WORK	OL	E
1 Preparation	OL	E
Introducing and discussing the topic		
Analysing the model for the project		
Going through the *How to* tips		
Clarifying the project		
2 Development	OL	E
Assigning roles and responsibilities		
Researching and analysing		
Drafting and reviewing		
3 Production	OL	E
Preparing the final presentation		
Presenting the project		
Reflecting on the process		

Kerr, Philip (2016). 'The learner's own language.' *Explorations in English Language and Linguistics*. 3.1:1-7.
Kerr, Philip (2014). *Translation and Own-language Activities*. Cambridge: Cambridge University Press.

MIXED ABILITIES IN PROJECT WORK

How can you teach in ways that suit each type of learner? Projects offer a great advantage in this area, as students can explore different ways of completing them.

Mixed-ability classes can have individual differences such as motivation, ability, age and experience. Allow your students to express their ideas in different ways, and remember that no one will be happy with a project that is too difficult or too easy.

Studies have shown that adolescence is the best time for instructed language learning. Teenagers are faster at learning and are ready to observe and use rules (DeKeyser, 2010)[1]. Your activities should reflect this, which means getting to know your students and their differences in the following four areas:

Cognitive maturity	**Proficiency**	**Interests**	**Learning preferences**
Your students' ages and experiences affect their ability to understand and follow instructions.	Every member of your class will have a different language level.	Teenagers have a wide variety of interests and skills.	Everyone has different learning preferences, such as reading, taking notes, asking questions, listening, moving around or watching videos.
Adapt instructions according to level and avoid complicated words and phrases with beginners and elementary students.	Make sure tasks involve an appropriate degree of difficulty and are suitably challenging. Provide the levels of support needed.	Allow students to take roles within a project that help them develop their personal interests and relate to the main task. Encourage them to expand their knowledge.	Use a variety of learning styles in your classroom, such as visual, kinaesthetic, auditory, multimodal or text.

The roles of the facilitator

Give feedback

Is it a mouse?

Ask for and give reasons

Why? Because ...

Encourage participation

What do you think?

Listen actively

That's interesting! Really?

[1] DeKeyser, R., Alfi-Shabtay, I., & Ravid, D. (2010). 'Cross-linguistic evidence for the nature of age effects in second language acquisition.' *Applied Psycholinguistics*, 31(3), 413-438.

Classroom suggestions

Challenge		Suggestion

Challenge	Suggestion
When working in groups, stronger students solve the problems, while others stay quiet.	Allow time for 'think, pair, share' activities, where students think individually first, discuss ideas with a partner, then share with another pair.
When weaker students are put in groups according to ability, they become labelled as 'less proficient', which affects their motivation and self-esteem.	Change groups to make sure all students benefit and contribute in different contexts.
High-ability students do not feel challenged.	Give extension work and higher-level input.
Weaker students do not complete tasks.	Give additional support and adapted activities.

Differentiated instruction

We provide a specific suggestion for differentiated instruction in each project. Each one has three categories:

1 *Support* activities help students to better understand the tasks and concepts

2 *Consolidation* activities reinforce what students are learning

3 *Extension* activities provide additional challenges for stronger students.

1 PREPARATION		
Support	**Consolidation**	**Extension**
Suggest ways to record and keep notes. Extend time limits. Give specific goals related to competencies.	Have students organise ideas. Provide specific tasks to improve competencies. Give extra roles and responsibilities.	Suggest alternative ideas. Focus on additional competencies. Set additional goals.

2 DEVELOPMENT		
Support	**Consolidation**	**Extension**
Provide more examples of models. Suggest sources for research. Give essential information that helps with students' roles. Ask specific questions about findings.	Analyse different models. Have students share opinions. Make additional notes of findings. Check sources. Give extra responsibility in line with roles.	Produce another model for the project. Analyse opinions. Look for different points of view. Allow for peer-teaching.

3 PRODUCTION		
Support	**Consolidation**	**Extension**
Ensure level-appropriate participation during presentation. Allow feedback in own language. Suggest ways to improve.	Encourage feedback in English. Have students discuss self-evaluation. Encourage suggestions for ways to improve.	Give all feedback and evaluation in English. Have students interview each other about what they learned. Encourage suggestions for ways to improve.

TIME MANAGEMENT IN PROJECT WORK

① Be prepared

Take a look at the project before you start the unit.

② Divide the project into smaller tasks

Every project is made of a number of smaller tasks, such as research, preparation, organising notes and brainstorming. Ask yourself:

- *How long will each task take?*
- *Can the task be done in class or out of class?*
- *At what stage of the unit can students complete each step?*
- *What language do they need?*

By approaching the project this way, you will see that the steps may not take up too much class time.

③ Prioritise and set short-term goals

Think about how the project groups can best use class time. Should they brainstorm, draw pictures or organise sentences? Be clear about what you want the groups to achieve by the end of each session.

It is important that groups present their projects when they expect to do so. It can be demotivating if you run out of time before they present.

④ Help students plan out-of-class assignments

Ensure the groups understand that the out-of-class tasks are just as important as the in-class ones when preparing a project. Set goals and give time limits. Encourage them to use their My time-management plans when you see this icon: ⏰

> My time-management plan p71

⑤ Be flexible between projects

How much time you give students for each task will vary from project to project. It may depend on factors such as previous knowledge, level of language difficulty or access to information.

⑥ Set a time for the presentation

Make sure you allow sufficient class time for the presentation step, including its evaluation. If the steps leading to the final product have been distributed and completed in an organised way, it's likely there will be more time for presenting it.

CHALLENGES AND IMPLICATIONS

As it is their second year, most of your students are now familiar with the school environment and have experience of working in groups. While many will still prefer to work individually, they will have also seen the benefits of a well-organised project group.

Your second-year students will continue to go through social, emotional and physiological changes. Also, they will probably have more responsibilities and academic pressure.

What are some changes and challenges to expect?

Change	Challenge
Academic: more workload and responsibilities	organising time, planning when to study, doing homework, staying motivated
Environment: different teachers and expectations	getting used to new ways of learning, building trust
Social: new friends or social groups (some students will change friends or clubs)	dealing with peer pressure, resolving conflicts, building good relations
Self growth: physiological, emotional and moral changes	building self-confidence, developing empathy, providing emotional support
Personal: more complex personal issues, new interests	sharing personal problems, maintaining open communication

All these changes and their challenges have implications for how to use project work in your classroom. You can encourage successful collaboration by:

- describing how you are going to organise your classes

- explaining how much guidance you will give, and your expectations

- making students feel excited about how they can work (using the internet, online programs, library, etc.)

- observing group dynamics

- organising group work from the start

- making sure no one is isolated

- developing different skills through different ways of working (e.g. reflection, peer-evaluation, listening to others)

- continuing to pay attention to each student as an individual.

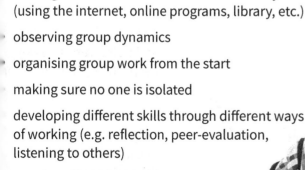
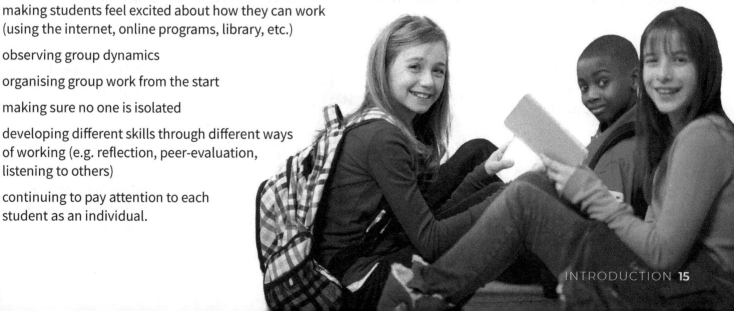

COLLABORATION

Collaborative skills	Behaviours	Level 2 Projects
Peer-tutoring	Correcting and editing each other's work	**A storyboard for an advert:** match the script with the images; check content; suggest additions
Giving constructive feedback	Commenting on group members' work	**A museum display:** give positive feedback and suggest improvements to each other's sections
Resolving conflicts	Reaching a compromise and making final decisions	**A comic strip:** choose a story; agree on key events; select the best way to represent events
Using social skills	Giving opinions, persuading, compromising, agreeing	**A poster:** agree on content; express opinions politely
Encouraging responsibility	Completing tasks on time to finish a project together	**A poster:** find information individually; prepare own section; check each other's work
Listening actively	Responding to others' work or suggestions	**An information leaflet:** plan information together; share first drafts and give opinions
Disagreeing appropriately	Giving opinions politely to come to a solution	**A 3D room plan:** decide on modern technology and furniture; comment on labels and diagrams
Sharing tasks	Making sure all group members have a task and role	**A timeline:** identify the main tasks and roles; set long-term and short-term deadlines; review the project regularly
Sharing resources	Helping group members to complete or improve work	**A webpage:** find and share online templates, images and information; help each other find these resources

Roles and responsibilities

Each project has specific roles; however, here are some general roles that you can apply at any time.

The **group leader** supervises, communicates with the teacher and manages participation.

The **resource manager** looks after resources and keeps the final product for presentation.

The **diary keeper** records decisions and tracks roles and responsibilities.

The **inspector** checks and edits information.

The **coordinator** tracks time and makes sure individuals complete their tasks.

The flipped classroom

Project work and the flipped classroom

During

IN CLASS

Put together work, edit, share opinions, present, give feedback, peer-evaluate

LEARNING OUTCOMES → LEARNING OUTCOMES → LEARNING OUTCOMES →

OUT OF CLASS

Before

Research, interview, prepare reports, make illustrations, organise sentences

After

Complete learning diaries, reflect, self-evaluate

Each project in this book contains at least one flipped classroom idea. Students are still collaborating when they use this approach. They have to share roles, get things ready on time, share information and resources and check one another's work. Students should plan out-of-class project work and use their My time-management plans. **> My time-management plan p71**

How well did I collaborate?

At the end of the process, have students answer a few questions about how well they collaborated.

Did I ...
help my group?
share information?
do the tasks for my role?

Was I motivated?

Did we ...
trust each other in my group?
share opinions in my group?
share materials in my group?

What can I do to be a better group member?

PRESENTATION IDEAS

The end goal of project work is the presentation step. This is when students are able to show their final product and how they have achieved their learning outcomes.

As well as being a natural way to end the project process, this stage also gives you an opportunity to check students' progress in the foundational layers of the Cambridge Life Competencies Framework. **> Cambridge Life Competencies Framework p6**

FOUNDATION LAYERS	ABILITIES	EXAMPLE ACTIONS
Emotional Development and Wellbeing	• Identify and understand emotions • Manage emotions • Empathise and build relationships	reflecting on strengths and weaknesses, verbalising emotions, employing coping mechanisms, adapting to stressful emotions, caring for others
Digital Literacy	• Use digital tools	creating documents, collaborating, sharing work, finding content, following safe practices
Discipline Knowledge	• Convince the audience	giving details, using facts and logic, demonstrating knowledge, summarising information, answering questions

Here are a few practical considerations when facilitating the presentation stage.

✓ Allow students enough time to prepare.

✓ Make sure students support each other – particularly shy students – before, during and after the presentation.

✓ Remind students of the learning outcomes and *why* they are presenting.

✓ Give students a reason for listening to presentations (peer-evaluation) and leave time for questions and discussion.

The following page gives ideas for ways to present some of the Level 2 projects. However, they are only suggestions. Where possible, let students choose modes of presentation that are most suitable for their projects and the classroom context.

1 Storyboards

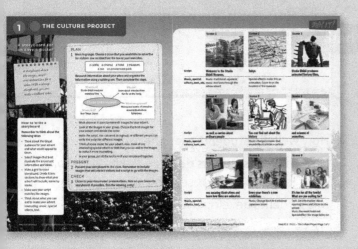

Have students use word-processing programs to make storyboards and room plans online.

2 Room plans

1. **Choose** an area. Draw an outline and take measurements.

2. **Add** fixed features (doors, windows, sinks ...)

3. **Add** furniture. Use simple shapes.

4. **Label** the plan. Add descriptions in call-out boxes where necessary.

5. **Check** spelling and grammar. Make sure the room plan is easy to understand.

3 Walk-in displays

1 **Look at** an example of a **walk-in display** (show students the elements of a walk-in display).

2 **Research** more examples of walk-in displays and have students make their own drawings.

3 **Choose** a favourite display and have students arrange their projects in a similar way.

4 **Make sure** students look at the projects in a logical order.

5 **Invite** students to walk around and look at each other's projects.

EVALUATION

What?

Product

How well did students achieve their **learning outcomes**?

How well did they demonstrate these?

How did they **evaluate options** and make **decisions**?

Process

How well did students **plan** the product?

How well did students **develop** the project (roles and responsibilities, research and analysis)?

Did students develop **life competencies**?

Who?

Self-evaluation	Peer-evaluation	Teacher–student evaluation

When?

Preparation

After groups are formed: checking learning outcomes, brainstorming ideas, identifying key information, making decisions about content

Development

After each step: thinking about roles and responsibilities, researching and analysing findings, drafting and reviewing

Production

Before presentation: deciding how to present

During presentation: practising presentation skills

After: giving feedback and self-evaluating

How?

Informal evaluation tools

KWL chart, My learning diary, Peer-evaluation form

> Evaluation tools pp67–69

Formal evaluation tools

Project evaluation rubrics, evaluation rubric, teacher's evaluation form

> Evaluation rubric p21

> Teacher's evaluation form p70

EVALUATION RUBRIC

The rubric below covers areas you can evaluate in every project. You can select some or all of these for each project when you feel it is necessary. There are also two project-specific rubrics with adapted evaluation descriptors in each unit.

Exceeds expectations (4): students show they are ready to go further and can take extra challenges in certain areas.

Very good (3): students complete the tasks successfully and as expected.

Good (2): students complete the tasks reasonably well with some aspects done better than others.

Needs improvement (1): students show room for improvement in most areas evaluated.

	4	3	2	1
Learning outcomes	Completes all stages to successfully achieve the overall learning outcomes.	Completes most stages effectively. Largely achieves overall learning outcomes.	Has missed some stages. Partially completes overall learning outcomes.	Hasn't successfully completed any of the stages. Overall learning outcomes unachieved.
Planning and organisation	Product is well organised, interesting and easy to follow. It follows the model for the project and no details are missing.	Product is well organised and easy to follow. Some details are incorrect or missing.	Product is similar to the model for the project, but is missing essential information. It follows the model with difficulty.	Product does not look or sound anything like the one in the task. There is little or no sequence to ideas.
Use of information and resources	Uses a wide range of resources to get information about the product.	Uses different resources to get information with some gaps.	Most information is useful, but only comes from one or two resources.	There is little evidence of research and hasn't used appropriate resources.
Collaboration (Teamwork)	Collaborated in all stages and understood roles and responsibilities.	Collaborated in all stages and understood responsibilities. There was minor confusion about roles and responsibilities.	Collaborated in most stages but there was some confusion about roles and responsibilities.	There was little or no collaboration throughout all stages. Didn't recognise roles and responsibilities.
Time management	Completed everything on time. Revised and corrected project.	Completed everything on time, with one or two steps at the last minute. Revised and corrected project.	Completed all steps, but at the last minute. There was little time for revision or correction.	Did not finish project. Missed steps in the process.
Creativity	Product is very original and interesting. All ideas are well developed.	Product is interesting and very creative. Most ideas are well developed.	There is some evidence of creativity which could have been developed. Product is a mixture of original and copied ideas.	Little imagination or creativity. Most ideas copied and pasted from other sources.
Problem-solving skills	All group members participate and listen actively to solve problems effectively at all times.	Most group members are actively involved to solve most problems.	Some evidence of problem-solving but not by all group members.	Little or no evidence of problem-solving, either individually or in groups.
Language use	Excellent use of language. Project is clear and understandable with only a few mistakes.	Good use of language. Project is clear and understandable with some mistakes.	Adequate use of language. Project is understandable, but some sections need further explanation.	Random words are used in a confusing way. Project is almost impossible to understand.
Presentation skills	All group members participate. Presentation is well put-together and is clear and interesting throughout.	All group members participate. Presentation is mostly clear and interesting.	All group members participate, but the method of presentation is sometimes inappropriate or not engaging.	None of the group members fully participate. Inappropriate and uninteresting method of presentation.
Final product	Exceeds expectations.	Very good.	Good.	Needs improvement.

A STORYBOARD FOR AN ADVERT

- **Learning outcome:** make a storyboard for an advert
- **Skills:** research information and make a spidergram to organise it, research and choose images for an advert, write a script
- **Resources:** two or more short video adverts for places, Storyboard organiser p58, My time-management plan p71
- **Evaluation tools:** Project evaluation rubric p25, My learning diary p68, Peer-evaluation form p69, Teacher's evaluation form p70

 Unit 1

Before you start

Find two or three video adverts for places from the internet to show students in class.

① Preparation

Step 1: Introduce the topic

- Introduce the topic of adverts after doing the vocabulary exercises. 📖 p11 Ask: *What do TV channels show between programmes? What types of things do adverts show?*

- Show students the video adverts. Encourage them to say what they are for and what they see in each scene. Ask: *What is the purpose of the advert? Is it a good advert? Why / Why not?*

- Discuss where we can find adverts (online, in magazines, on TV, etc.). Explain that adverts give information about products or places to get people to buy things or visit places.

- Ask students to bring an example of a video advert for a place to the next class (in their own language or English). They can discuss them and say whether they'd like to visit the place and why.

Step 2: Analyse the model for the project Unit 1

- Look at the model storyboard with the class. Ask: *Which place is the storyboard about? What sections can you see? (Images, scenes, script, music, special effects and text.) What is interesting? Would you like to visit this place?*

- Ask students to imagine the advert this storyboard is for. They could suggest extra ideas to include.

Creative Thinking
Creating new content from own ideas or other resources

Monitor students' participation during the class discussion in Step 2.

Step 3: *How to* write a storyboard 🖱 Unit 1

- Go through the first two *How to* tips with the class. Say it is important to know who the target audience is (for example, children, teenagers or adults) so that the information in the advert appeals to them.

- Discuss where students can find suitable images. Explain that for storyboards, it is also common to sketch images before finding them.

- Go through the rest of the tips. Check that students understand that when they make their storyboards, they should use the ideas in this *How to* section.

Step 4: Clarify the project 🖱 Unit 1

- Follow the steps in > The learning stages of project work p10.
- Brainstorm different places from around the world to advertise.
- Have groups discuss why each place is interesting and what information they can put in an advert about it.

> My learning diary p68 **Preparation**

> Peer-evaluation form p69 **Preparation**

② Development

Start this stage as soon as groups know their learning outcomes and have brainstormed places to advertise.

Step 1: Assign roles and responsibilities

- In project groups, have students decide on general roles. > Roles and responsibilities p16 Help them decide on further roles they can share, such as the ones in the diagram.

The **special effects coordinator** suggests special effects.

The **picture manager** helps choose the images.

The **scriptwriter** checks that the script is correct for each scene and suggests improvements.

The **music supervisor** helps choose the music.

The **artist** helps sketch the ideas.

Step 2: Research and analyse 🖱 Unit 1 ⏰ p71

- Have groups do the first part of the PLAN section from **Exercise 1**. Have them choose a place from the ones they brainstormed or think of a different one, using the ideas from the box.

- Point to the model spidergram and ask what type of information it has.

↻ Flipped classroom activity

Out of class: have students research information about their place, using the questions in the model spidergram and organising their notes into a similar spidergram. Have them also find images.

In class: group members compare their findings. Ask: *Who is your target audience? Are the images useful?* Students choose the best information and images for their storyboard.

Step 3: Draft and review Unit 1 p71

- Hand out a copy of the > Storyboard organiser p58 to each student.

- Group members complete the last four points of the PLAN section. Ask them to sketch or place their ideas in their organisers. Give each member of the group an image or two to write the script for.

↻ Flipped classroom activity

Out of class: in their organisers, students write the scripts for their part of the storyboard (alternatively, groups can work together on the whole script in class). Encourage them to describe their images using the **present simple** and **present continuous**.

In class: group members work together to make notes about music, special effects and any other features. Then they put their storyboards together and review them.

🛡 Learning to Learn
Reflecting on and evaluating own learning success

Monitor progress of the tasks in Steps 2 and 3, checking that group members use their spidergrams and organisers effectively. (See Differentiated instruction activities below for further practice.)

Differentiated instruction

Support
Help students review their storyboard section, checking it contains all the necessary information.
Consolidation
Encourage students to check each other's scripts. Suggest moving text around to match images.
Extension
Allow students to make final decisions on the order of the images, as well as on the script, music and special effects.

> My learning diary p68 **Development**

> Peer-evaluation form p69 **Development**

③ Production

Schedule presentation times and stick to them, so that each group can present their storyboards. Spread the presentations over a few classes, if necessary. Allow enough time for each presentation and for questions.

Before groups present their final storyboards, check that they have followed and completed the steps.

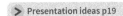 Presentation ideas p19

As students complete their projects, check their abilities in the following Competencies.

Creative Thinking
Creating new content from own ideas or other resources

Communicates personal response to creative work from art, music or literature.

Evidence: Students look at different storyboards and vote for the best one.

Learning to Learn
Reflecting on and evaluating own learning success

Selects and uses a wide range of mind maps and other tools to organise thoughts.

Evidence: Students use their spidergrams and storyboard organisers to put together key information.

Identifies what needs to be revisited before identifying new learning goals.

Evidence: Group members check each other's work and suggest improvements.

Step 1: Prepare ⬤ Unit 1 ⏰ p71

- Go through the PRESENT section in **Exercise 2**.

- As groups prepare their project, ask questions, for example: *Does the script match the images? Are there ideas for music and special effects? What else can you add?*

- Check grammar and spelling. Remind students to use the present simple for facts and the present continuous for actions in progress.

- Remind groups of the presentation date and how much time each group will have.

⌂ *Own it!* learning tip

Peer-tutoring

Monitor group members as they correct and edit each other's work. Explain that this includes checking spelling, punctuation and language as well as checking that the scripts and extra features match the images. Encourage students to suggest improvements or additions to each other's work and make changes where necessary. Help with useful language, for example: *Why don't you … ? You could … Maybe you should change this.*

Step 2: Present ⬤ Unit 1

- Draw attention to the CHECK section in **Exercise 3**. Ask the class to check each group's storyboards. Have them write down any interesting facts.

- Have groups present their storyboards. Remind speakers to explain their section, describing each image and saying how the script relates to it.

Step 3: Reflect ⬤ Unit 1

- After all the presentations, hold a class vote on the best storyboard.

- Discuss different steps of the project process and the final result. Ask: *How well did you work in your group? What did you find difficult / interesting? Would you like to visit any of the places?*

- Have students vote on their favourite storyboard.

- If possible, have the winning group film their advert, using the images they found, recording their script and adding the music and special effects. Suggest that they share roles, such as narrator, editor and director.

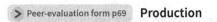 Peer-evaluation form p69   **Production**

⬤ Go to the digital collaboration space to set, track and assess students' work, or allow students to share and comment on their own work.

Project evaluation rubric: a storyboard for an advert

Use these project-specific descriptors and your choice of descriptors from the **> Evaluation rubric p21** to check students individually or in groups. Make your own evaluation form. **> Teacher's evaluation form p70**

	4	3	2	1
Creativity	Product is well organised with creative and interesting ideas. It shows attractive images in a logical order. It uses interesting scripts and includes all the extra features.	Product is organised with interesting ideas. It shows attractive images in a mostly logical order. It uses fairly interesting scripts and includes some of the extra features.	Product has interesting ideas but lacks organisation. It shows images in an order that is sometimes confusing. It uses scripts, though they're not very interesting, and includes very few extra features.	Product lacks interesting ideas and organisation. It shows images in a confusing order. The scripts aren't interesting and some are missing. There are no extra features.
Language use	Product shows excellent use of grammar, punctuation and spelling. Excellent use of language from unit (present simple and continuous). Project is understandable with only a few or no mistakes.	Product shows good use of grammar, punctuation and spelling. Good use of language from unit (present simple and continuous). Project is understandable with some mistakes.	Product shows adequate use of grammar, punctuation and spelling. Adequate use of language from unit (present simple and continuous). Project is understandable, but some sections need further explanation.	Product shows poor use of grammar, punctuation and spelling. Poor or no use of language from unit (present simple and continuous). Project is confusing and almost impossible to understand.

 Cambridge Life Competencies Framework
You can also check students' progress in the following foundation layers.

FOUNDATION LAYERS	ABILITIES	ACTIONS
Digital Literacy	• Use digital tools	finding content on various websites, downloading images, sharing work online, assessing online material
Discipline Knowledge	• Convince the audience	presenting ideas, summarising information, describing images, explaining the extra features, answering questions

○ Flipped classroom activities

Evaluate

In project groups, have students discuss their completed Peer-evaluation forms and ways to work better as a group. **> Peer-evaluation form p69**

Out of class: have students think about their progress at home. **> My learning diary p68** **Production**

In class: discuss what students learned using the information from their learning diaries.
> My learning diary p68 **Production**

2 THE HISTORY PROJECT

A MUSEUM DISPLAY

- **Learning outcome:** design a museum display of historical objects

- **Skills:** research historical objects and find images, write texts about the objects, correct facts and dates, give feedback on the other groups' displays

- **Resources:** examples of museum displays, Museum display organiser p59, My time-management plan p71

- **Evaluation tools:** Project evaluation rubric p29, KWL chart p67, Peer-evaluation form p69, Teacher's evaluation form p70

Student's Book pp30–31

Before you start

Find two or three examples of museum displays from the internet to show students in class. Check that the examples show different ways of presenting information (through text, pictures, interactive presentations, etc.).

1 Preparation

Step 1: Introduce the topic

- Introduce the topic of museum displays after doing the radio programme listening exercises. p26

- Show students the examples of museum displays. Encourage them to say what they are and what their purpose is. Ask: *Why do people visit museums? Which museums do you visit and why? What can you see in museums? What do these displays use to present the exhibits? (Photos, descriptions, dates, etc.)*

- Explain that museum displays give information about exhibits. Ask: *What makes a good museum display?* Say that good displays give visitors an experience they can remember.

- Ask students to bring an image of a museum display to the next class. Discuss which displays they like most and why.

Step 2: Analyse the model for the project pp30–31

- Complete **Exercises 1** to **3**.

Answers **1** Students' own answers **2** 2 M **3** L **4** S **5** B **6** M **7** L **8** B
3 Students' own answers

- Ask questions about the model museum displays, for example: *Do they give interesting information? What types of facts are in the texts? How do the photos help? Does the design look good? Why / Why not?*

- Revise the language from the unit. Ask students to find examples of the **past simple**. Ask why the texts use this tense (to narrate past events and describe how people used these objects in the past).

Step 3: *How to* give feedback p30

- 🎧 2.11 Go through the *How to* tips in **Exercise 4** with the class. Then play the audio to check answers.

Answers The Mexican bowl and the bronze lamps.

- 🎧 2.11 Play the audio again for **Exercise 5**. Encourage discussion of question 5 and list ideas on the board.

Answers **5 1** It was interesting and she learned something new. **2** Making the final sentence two sentences. **3** Do more research and include more information. **4** and **5** Students' own answers

- Check students understand that when they give feedback, they should use the ideas in this *How to* section.

Step 4: Clarify the project pp30–31

- Follow the steps in > The learning stages of project work p10 . For this project, we suggest students work in groups of four.

- Brainstorm a list of historical objects. Groups discuss what visitors would like to know about each of the objects.

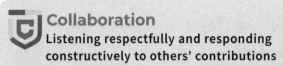

Collaboration
Listening respectfully and responding constructively to others' contributions
Monitor how well students listen and respond to each other during the discussions in Steps 2, 3 and 4.

> KWL chart p67 **Know and Want to know**

> Peer-evaluation form p69 **Preparation**

② Development

Start this stage as soon as groups know their learning outcomes and are ready to choose four objects from their brainstormed lists.

Step 1: Assign roles and responsibilities

- In project groups, have students decide on general roles. > Roles and responsibilities p16 Help them decide on further roles they can share. Draw a diagram like this on the board:

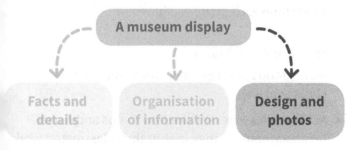

- Ask questions related to each section in the diagram. Discuss the tasks and roles needed to create a museum display:

Facts and details: *Where can you find information about the objects? How can you check that the facts are correct? What sources will you use? Who will help decide on important facts and details?*

Organisation of information: *What is the main idea for each text? What are the supporting ideas? Who will help organise the information?*

Design and photos: *How will you make the display look good? Where can you find images? Who will help choose the images?*

- Encourage students to take notes and decide on roles.

Step 2: Research and analyse 📖 p31 ⏰ p71

- Hand out a copy of the > Museum display organiser p59 to each student.

- Have each student choose an object to research. Help students choose different objects within each group.

⟳ Flipped classroom activity

Out of class: have group members complete the first part of the PLAN section from **Exercise 6**. Tell them to research their object and write the information in their organiser.

Have them also find images.

In class: have group members check their work together and suggest improvements.

Step 3: Draft and review 📖 p31 ⏰ p71

- Have groups complete the PLAN section from **Exercise 6**. They put their museum display together using the ideas from their organisers.

- Encourage students to make last-minute revisions. Remind them to check the use of the past simple for narrating past events.

🛡 Communication
Managing conversations

Monitor the conversations in the groups as they put together their project. Check that group members are making suggestions and responding constructively to each other's ideas.

⌂ *Own it!* learning tip

Giving constructive feedback

Remind students of the three steps for giving feedback: say something positive, say something you think is weak and suggest an improvement. Encourage students to follow this structure as they comment on and put together their work. Help them with useful language, for example: *That's a good idea! This works well. I'm not sure this works. I think we can make this better. Why don't you ... ?*

> Peer-evaluation form p69 **Development**

3 Production

Schedule presentation times and stick to them. Remember that these projects will be put on the classroom wall. Allow enough time for students to look at all the museum displays, ask questions and give feedback.

Before groups produce their final drafts, have them look at different examples of museum displays again. Help them with ideas for how to present their information logically.

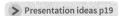 Presentation ideas p19

As students complete their projects, check their abilities in the following Competencies.

Collaboration
Listening respectfully and responding constructively to others' contributions

Listens to / acknowledges different points of view respectfully.

Evidence: Groups respond respectfully to each other's feedback.

Evaluates contributions from other students with appropriate sensitivity.

Evidence: If groups disagree with feedback, they do it in a polite way.

Communication
Managing conversations

Can use simple techniques to start, maintain and close conversations of various lengths.

Evidence: Students give feedback on and answer questions about each other's displays.

Uses appropriate strategies to develop a conversation (e.g. showing interest).

Evidence: Students give feedback on each other's displays.

Step 1: Prepare 📖 p31 ⏰ p71

- Go through the PRESENT section in **Exercise 7**.
- As groups prepare their project, ask questions, for example: *Are the facts and dates correct? What images are you using? Do the texts match them? What can you do to improve the design?*
- Check the use of the past simple in the texts. Allow time for final corrections.
- Remind groups of the presentation date and how much time each group will have.

Step 2: Present 📖 pp30–31

- Have groups put their museum displays on the classroom wall.
- Ask the class to review the *How to* tips and make feedback notes as they look at their classmates' work.
- Groups walk around, looking at the museum displays and writing their comments.
- Draw attention to the CHECK section in **Exercise 8**. Have groups give feedback to each other using their notes. Monitor the progress of this task.

Step 3: Reflect 📖 p31

- After the feedback session, encourage students to think about each stage of the project process, including positive experiences and things they could improve. (See Differentiated instruction activities below for further practice.)

Differentiated instruction

Support
Have students vote on the best display and share the result with the class.

Consolidation
Have pairs list the strong and weak elements of one of the displays and share their ideas with the group that designed it.

Extension
In project groups, students write three questions about interesting facts from their display. Then pairs of groups quiz each other.

> Peer-evaluation form p69 **Production**

 Go to the digital collaboration space to set, track and assess students' work, or allow students to share and comment on their own work.

Project evaluation rubric: a museum display

Use these project-specific descriptors and your choice of descriptors from the **> Evaluation rubric p21** to check students individually or in groups. Make your own evaluation form. **> Teacher's evaluation form p70**

	4	3	2	1
Creativity	Product is well organised and has a very attractive design. It uses interesting and appropriate images. It has clear information, including accurate facts from reliable sources.	Product is well organised and has an attractive design. It uses appropriate images, and some of them are interesting. It has mostly clear information, including accurate facts from reliable sources.	Product is organised and has a clear but not very attractive design. It uses appropriate images, but they are not interesting. It has accurate information from reliable sources, but very few facts are clear.	Product is poorly organised and has an unattractive design. It has few or no images, and none of them are appropriate or interesting. It doesn't have clear or accurate information.
Language use	Excellent use of language from unit (past simple). Project is understandable with only a few mistakes.	Good use of language from unit (past simple). Project is understandable with some mistakes.	Adequate use of language from unit (past simple). Project is understandable, but some sections need further explanation.	Poor or no use of language from unit (past simple). Project is confusing and almost impossible to understand.

 Cambridge Life Competencies Framework

You can also check students' progress in the following foundation layers.

FOUNDATION LAYERS	ABILITIES	ACTIONS
Emotional Development and Wellbeing	• Manage emotions	making helpful suggestions, giving constructive feedback, responding to feedback respectfully
Discipline Knowledge	• Convince the audience	explaining facts and images, giving details, summarising information, narrating past events, answering questions

↻ Flipped classroom activities

Evaluate

In project groups, have students discuss their completed Peer-evaluation forms and ways to work better as a group. **> Peer-evaluation form p69**

Out of class: have students think about their progress at home. **> KWL chart p67** **Learned**

In class: discuss what students learned, using the information from their KWL charts. **> KWL chart p67** **Learned**

A COMIC STRIP

- **Learning outcome:** make a comic strip

- **Skills:** identify the key events in a traditional story, sequence events, brainstorm and draw images to represent each event, add text, present the comic strip

- **Resources:** two or more comic strips, Comic strip organiser p60, My time-management plan p71

- **Evaluation tools:** Project evaluation rubric p33, My learning diary p68, Peer-evaluation form p69, Teacher's evaluation form p70

 Unit 3

Before you start

Collect two or three different comic strips to show students in class.

① Preparation

Step 1: Introduce the topic

- Introduce the topic of comic strips after doing the writing exercises. p41 By this time, students will have seen a number of different text types for telling stories. Alternatively, you could introduce the topic earlier, after doing the reading exercises. 📖 p36
Ask: *Do you read comic strips? What comic strips do you like? Where do you find them?*

- Show students the comic strips. Ask: *What are the different parts of comic strips?* Point out how comic strips are divided into panels using images, close-ups, speech and thought bubbles. Ask what each element is for.

- Explain that a comic strip is a sequence of drawings which tell a story. Say that comic strips use speech bubbles for dialogue and other types of bubbles for thoughts and noises.

- Ask students to bring a comic strip to the next class (in their own language or English). They can describe the images and story, and say what they like about them.

Step 2: Analyse the model for the project Unit 3

- Draw attention to the title of the model comic strip and ask students what they think the story is about. Then have students identify the key event in each picture.

- Explain that the story is an adaptation of the Turkish fairytale *The boy who found fear*. Ask: *What is the boy afraid of at the end of the story? (Becoming the king.)*

- Ask further questions, for example: *What speech bubbles can you see? Why is 'Help!' in a different-shaped bubble? Do you like the story and pictures? What can you add?*

- In pairs, have students tell the story by looking at the pictures.

Step 3: *How to* make a comic strip Unit 3

- Go through the *How to* tips with the class. Students look at the model strip to see how the tips have been followed.

- Check students understand that when they make their comic strips, they should use the ideas in this *How to* section.

Critical Thinking
Synthesising ideas and information
Monitor students' understanding of the key events in the model and how they are shown in comic strip format. Ask if there are other ways to narrate events.

Step 4: Clarify the project Unit 3

- Follow the steps in 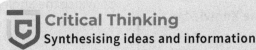 The learning stages of project work p10 .

- Brainstorm traditional stories from around the world.

- Have groups discuss which stories they like and what they know about them and the characters.

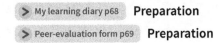
> My learning diary p68 **Preparation**
> Peer-evaluation form p69 **Preparation**

2 Development

Start this stage as soon as groups know their learning outcomes and have brainstormed traditional stories to research.

Step 1: Assign roles and responsibilities

- In project groups, have students decide on general roles. **>** Roles and responsibilities p16 Help them decide on further roles they can share, such as the ones in the diagram.

The **editor** helps put the events into the correct sequence.

The **proofreader** checks the text in the speech bubbles is correct.

The **writer** helps summarise the key events.

The **designer** suggests ideas for the layout of the panels.

The **art director** suggests ideas for the drawings/ images.

Step 2: Research and analyse Unit 3 p71

- Have groups start the PLAN section from **Exercise 1**. They choose a story from those they brainstormed.

- Groups pull out the key events in their story and write a list (with a maximum of 12 events), similar to the one in the PLAN section. Remind students to use the present simple when writing their lists.

  Hand out a copy of the **>** Comic strip organiser p60 to each student.

Step 3: Draft and review Unit 3 p71

Have groups brainstorm ideas for images to represent the key events. They can write their ideas in their organisers.

Tell groups to check each member has an equal number of images to draw.

Flipped classroom activity

Out of class: have students continue with the PLAN section at home. Ask them to draw their images in the Comic strip organiser. Remind them to present the key events in sequence.

In class: have groups cut out their drawings and arrange them in order on a desk or sheet of paper.

Groups prepare a final version of their comic strip on a piece of card and add text. Make sure groups agree on the number and order of key events. (See Differentiated instruction activities below for further practice.)

Differentiated instruction

Support
Help students with ideas for phrasing and sequencing key events, and with grammar tenses.
Consolidation
Encourage students to write dialogue and use speech and thought bubbles.
Extension
Have students come up with alternative endings for their comic strips. Encourage them to check each other's comic strips and choose their favourite.

Social Responsibilities
Taking active roles including leadership

Encourage all group members to participate and make decisions about different aspects of their comic strips in line with their roles.

> My learning diary p68 **Development**

> Peer-evaluation form p69 **Development**

③ Production

Schedule presentation times and stick to them, checking that all groups present their comic strips. Spread the presentations over a few classes, if necessary. Allow time for each presentation and for questions.

As groups produce their final drafts, you can remind them to follow the same steps as those for creating their storyboard in Unit 1. Groups may also want to create a digital version of their comic strip, using a free online comic strip maker.

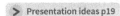 Presentation ideas p19

As students complete their projects, check their abilities in the following Competencies.

> ### Critical Thinking
> **Synthesising ideas and information**
>
> *Selects key points from diverse sources to create a new account.*
>
> Evidence: Students decide on and draw the key events in their stories.
>
> ### Social Responsibilities
> **Taking active roles including leadership**
>
> *In group work, makes consultative decisions.*
>
> Evidence: Students consider each other's ideas before making final decisions.
>
> *Encourages others to participate and contribute in projects.*
>
> Evidence: All group members take part in the project.

Step 1: Prepare Unit 3 p71

- Go through the PRESENT section in **Exercise 2**.

- As groups prepare their project, suggest that each member presents the panels they drew.

- Have group members practise their presentation. Remind them to use the pictures as prompts to tell the story, and include all the key events. Check students are using the **past simple** and **continuous** correctly when narrating the actions.

🔄 *Own it!* learning tip

Resolving conflicts

Encourage students to try to agree when making final decisions about the layout and text in their comic strip. If group members cannot come to an agreement, ask: *Can you think of an alternative / any solutions?* Have students listen actively and respond respectfully to each other's ideas. Help them with useful language, for example: *I think … Why don't we …? That's a good idea, but … What about … ?* Encourage students to learn how to agree when working in project groups.

Step 2: Present Unit 3

- Draw attention to the CHECK section in **Exercise 3**. Ask the class to think about these questions as they listen to each other's presentations.

- Have groups present their comic strips. Tell the class to make notes about what they like and why.

- Remind speakers to point to the pictures as they describe them. Encourage them to use different tones of voice for the narrator and characters' speech.

Step 3: Reflect Unit 3

- After the presentations, ask the class to decide on their favourite comic strips.

- As students discuss their favourite comic strip, ask: *Were the stories interesting? What did you like about the images? Were the key events easy to follow? Why / Why not?*

- Encourage students to think about each stage of the project process, including positive experiences and things they could improve.

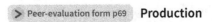 Peer-evaluation form p69   **Production**

🔄 Go to the digital collaboration space to set, track and assess students' work, or allow students to share and comment on their own work.

Project evaluation rubric: a comic strip

Use these project-specific descriptors and your choice of descriptors from the ▸ Evaluation rubric p21 to check students individually or in groups. Make your own evaluation form. ▸ Teacher's evaluation form p70

	4	3	2	1
Creativity	Product is interesting, attractive and easy to follow. It includes all the key events in the correct sequence. It has attractive images that match the events and help tell the story. It uses a variety of speech bubbles in an interesting way.	Product is interesting, attractive and fairly easy to follow. It includes most of the key events in the correct sequence. It has attractive images that usually match the events and help tell the story. It uses one type of speech bubble in an interesting way.	Product is fairly interesting and attractive, but not very easy to follow. It is missing some of the key events, and they aren't always in the correct sequence. It has images that usually match the events, but are not attractive. It is missing speech bubbles in some panels.	Product isn't interesting or attractive, and it is difficult to follow. It is missing many key events and the sequence is incorrect. The images don't match the events and aren't attractive. It is missing speech bubbles in most panels.
Language use	Product shows excellent use of grammar, punctuation and spelling. Excellent use of language from unit (past simple and continuous). Project is understandable with only a few or no mistakes.	Product shows good use of grammar, punctuation and spelling. Good use of language from unit (past simple and continuous). Project is understandable with some mistakes.	Product shows adequate use of grammar, punctuation and spelling. Adequate use of language from unit (past simple and continuous). Project is understandable, but some sections need further explanation.	Product shows poor use of grammar, punctuation and spelling. Poor or no use of language from unit (past simple and continuous). Project is confusing and almost impossible to understand.

 Cambridge Life Competencies Framework
You can also check students' progress in the following foundation layers.

FOUNDATION LAYERS	ABILITIES	ACTIONS
Discipline Knowledge	• Convince the audience	explaining key events clearly, using images to tell a story, using appropriate tone of voice when narrating a story
Emotional Development and Wellbeing	• Empathise and build relationships	listening actively, reaching compromises, reflecting on strengths and weaknesses, verbalising emotions appropriately, resolving conflicts

↻ Flipped classroom activities

Evaluate

In project groups, have students discuss their completed Peer-evaluation forms and ways to work better as a group. ▸ Peer-evaluation form p69

Out of class: have students think about their progress at home. ▸ My learning diary p68 **Production**

In class: discuss what students learned using the information from their learning diaries.
▸ My learning diary p68 **Production**

4 THE SOCIAL STUDIES PROJECT

A POSTER

- **Learning outcome:** make a poster
- **Skills:** ask for and express opinions to choose an idea, research information and photos about the idea, design the poster
- **Resources:** two or more posters about volunteer or community work, Poster organiser p61, My time-management plan p71
- **Evaluation tools:** Project evaluation rubric p37, KWL chart p67, Peer-evaluation form p69, Teacher's evaluation form p70

📖 Student's Book pp54–55

Before you start

Collect two or three different posters about volunteer or community work to show students in class.

1 Preparation

Step 1: Introduce the topic

- Introduce the topic of volunteer work after doing the listening exercises. 📖 p50
- Show students the posters. Ask: *What is the purpose of these posters? Where and when is the work? Why is this work necessary? Who can volunteer? What skills or interests do they need?*
- Explain that volunteering is an unpaid activity where someone gives their time to help a person, group or organisation. Ask: *What kind of volunteer work can teenagers do?* Write a list on the board. *(Clean up parks, work in an animal shelter, work in an old people's home.)*
- Ask students to bring a poster about volunteering to the next class. They can discuss the posters, saying which type of work they find interesting and why.

Step 2: Analyse the model for the project 📖 pp54–55

- Complete **Exercises 1 to 2.**

  Answers 1 b 2 1 Where? 2 What? 3 Who? 4 Why? 5 When? 6 What are the benefits?

- Ask questions about the model poster: *Is the message clear? Does the poster have all the key information? How does it present the information? Would you like to volunteer at the park? Why / Why not?*
- Revise the language from the unit. Ask students to find examples of **comparative and superlative adjectives, *can* and *could*,** and ***too much*** and ***(not) enough* + noun**.

🛡 Social Responsibilities
Understanding personal responsibilities as part of a group and in society

Have students discuss the poster message: *Together we can make our park better and cleaner!* Ask: *Why is volunteering important?* Discuss how volunteering helps the community.

Step 3: *How to* agree as a group 📖 p54

- Go through the *How to* tips in **Exercise 3** with the class. Check the answer.

  Possible answers 3 1 c 2 d 3 a 4 e 5 f 6 b

- 🎧 4.11 Tell the class that they will listen to three students talking about how to volunteer in their community. Play the audio for **Exercise 4** and check the answers. Play the audio again and have students identify words or phrases for suggesting ideas, interrupting politely and asking for or summing up opinions. *(Let's ... Excuse me ... Can I make a suggestion? What about ... ? Are there any more ideas? Right, so we all agree ...)*

  Answers 4 1 Lara; Thiago 2 Thiago 3 Yusuf

- Check students understand that when they need to agree as a group to make decisions, they should use the ideas in this *How to* section.

Step 4: Clarify the project 📖 pp54–55

- Follow the steps in 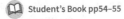 > The learning stages of project work p10 .
- Brainstorm different types of volunteer work and say how each type helps the community.

> KWL chart p67 **Know and Want to know**

> Peer-evaluation form p69 **Preparation**

② Development

Start this stage as soon as groups know their learning outcomes and have brainstormed different types of volunteer work.

Step 1: Assign roles and responsibilities

- In project groups, have students decide on general roles. > Roles and responsibilities p16 Help them decide on further roles they can share. Draw a diagram like this on the board:

- Ask questions related to each section in the diagram. Discuss the tasks and roles required to create a poster for volunteer work:

Message: *Who do you want to get as volunteers? What type of work is it? How can you make the work interesting? What information do people need? Who will help decide on the information to include?*

Organisation of information: *What information goes in the introduction? What sections will the poster have? Who will help organise the information?*

Design and photos: *How will you make the poster look good? Where can you find images? Who will help choose the images?*

- Encourage students to take notes and decide on roles.

Step 2: Research and analyse 📖 p55 ⏲ p71

- Have students read the ideas in the PLAN section from **Exercise 5** and choose a volunteer project. Alternatively, they can choose one idea from the list they brainstormed previously.

- Hand out a copy of the > Poster organiser p61 to each student.

Have group members think of messages to attract volunteers and complete the 'Introduction' part of their organisers.

○ Flipped classroom activity

Out of class: have students complete the rest of their organisers. Tell them to bring their ideas and researched photos to the next class.

In class: have group members compare their notes and photos. Give each group one more > Poster organiser p61 to complete with the best ideas and images.

Help groups agree on their final choices. They can refer to the ideas in the *How to* section. (See Differentiated instruction activities below for further practice.)

Differentiated instruction

Support
Help groups make decisions by giving them options. Help students sum up their ideas.

Consolidation
Allow students time to read the information in each other's organisers and come up with a list of final ideas.

Extension
Have group members lead the discussions about what to include and sum up the arguments for and against different options.

Creative Thinking
Using newly created content to solve problems

Monitor students as they plan their posters and look for original and creative ideas for attracting volunteers.

Step 3: Draft and review 📖 p55 ⏲ p71

- Hand out a piece of card to each group. They use the final ideas from their group Poster organiser to create a final version.

- Have students add the photos they chose and check language.

- Encourage students to look at each other's work and correct it. Check groups are using language from the unit in the texts.

> Peer-evaluation form p69   Development

③ Production

Schedule presentation times and stick to them. Remember that these projects will be displayed on the classroom wall. Allow enough time for students to look at all the posters, ask questions and give feedback.

Before groups produce their final drafts, have them look at different examples of posters again. Help them with ideas for how to arrange their information and present it logically.

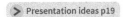 Presentation ideas p19

As students complete their projects, check their abilities in the following Competencies.

🛡 Social Responsibilities
Understanding personal responsibilities as part of a group and in society

Understands various aspects of society (e.g. volunteering).

Evidence: Poster shows why volunteers are needed.

Gets involved in collective action in the school (e.g. through volunteering).

Evidence: Poster shows how people can volunteer.

🛡 Creative Thinking
Using newly created content to solve problems

Employs new ideas and content in solving a task or activity.

Evidence: Poster has a creative design and interesting content.

Makes an assignment original by adding new angles.

Evidence: Poster mentions original reasons for volunteering.

Step 1: Prepare 📖 p55 ⏱ p71

- Go through the PRESENT section in **Exercise 6**.

- As groups prepare their project, ask questions, for example: *Is the information useful? How does the poster attract volunteers? What photos are you using? What things did you decide together as a group?*

- Remind groups of the presentation date and how much time each group will have.

🏠 *Own it!* learning tip

Using social skills

As groups finish their projects in Step 1, encourage them to use polite language for asking for and expressing opinions, interrupting politely and making decisions. Remind them of useful language, for example: *Let's … Excuse me … Can I make a suggestion? What about … ? Are there any more ideas? Right, so we all agree.*

Step 2: Present 📖 p55

- Draw attention to the CHECK section in **Exercise 7**. Ask the class to think about the question as they look at each other's posters.

- Have groups display their posters around the classroom.

- Ask students to walk around and look at the posters, tell them to decide which ones make them want to work as a volunteer.

- Encourage the class to ask questions and have group members say why and how their groups came to make some decisions.

Step 3: Reflect 📖 p55

- Write positive opinions about each poster on the board. Then have the class vote for the best poster and the best way to work as a volunteer in their community.

- Encourage students to think about each stage of the project process, including positive experiences and things they could improve.

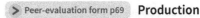 Peer-evaluation form p69 **Production**

 Go to the digital collaboration space to set, track and assess students' work, or allow students to share and comment on their own work.

Project evaluation rubric: a poster

Use these project-specific descriptors and your choice of descriptors from the ❯ Evaluation rubric p21 to check students individually or in groups. Make your own evaluation form. ❯ Teacher's evaluation form p70

	4	3	2	1
Creativity	Product is well organised with creative and interesting ideas. It has a lot of messages to attract volunteers. It uses attractive photos.	Product is organised with interesting ideas. It has some messages to attract volunteers. It uses some attractive photos.	Product has interesting ideas but lacks organisation. It has one or two messages to attract volunteers. It uses photos, but they aren't very attractive.	Product lacks interesting ideas and organisation. It doesn't have any messages to attract volunteers. It uses very few or no photos.
Language use	Product shows excellent use of grammar, punctuation and spelling. Excellent use of language from unit. Project is understandable with only a few or no mistakes.	Product shows good use of grammar, punctuation and spelling. Good use of language from unit. Project is understandable with some mistakes.	Product shows adequate use of grammar, punctuation and spelling. Adequate use of language from unit. Project is understandable, but some sections need further explanation.	Product shows poor use of grammar, punctuation and spelling. Poor or no use of language from unit. Project is confusing and almost impossible to understand.

 Cambridge Life Competencies Framework
You can also check students' progress in the following foundation layers.

FOUNDATION LAYERS	ABILITIES	ACTIONS
Emotional Development and Wellbeing	• Empathise and build relationships	expressing opinions and interrupting politely, making decisions and agreeing as a group, verbalising emotions appropriately
Discipline Knowledge	• Convince the audience	using persuasive language, demonstrating knowledge, giving details, answering questions

↻ Flipped classroom activities

Evaluate

In project groups, have students discuss their completed Peer-evaluation forms and ways to work better as a group. ❯ Peer-evaluation form p69

Out of class: have students think about their progress at home. ❯ KWL chart p67   **Learned**

In class: discuss what students learned, using the information from their KWL charts. ❯ KWL chart p67   **Learned**

A POSTER

- **Learning outcome:** design a poster
- **Skills:** find information about an unusual traditional home and use a spidergram to organise it, decide on a design including photos and maps, present the poster
- **Resources:** two or more posters, Poster organiser p62, My time-management plan p71
- **Evaluation tools:** Project evaluation rubric p41, My learning diary p68, Peer-evaluation form p69, Teacher's evaluation form p70

 Unit 5

Before you start

Collect two or three online or print posters about unusual traditional homes to show students in class. Choose those that have both graphics and written information about the home, such as its history, materials and location.

① Preparation

Step 1: Introduce the topic

- Introduce the topic of traditional homes after doing the reading exercises. p60 Ask: *Which home is your favourite? Why? How are these homes different from traditional ones?*

- Show students the posters. Ask: *What is the purpose of these posters? What can you learn about each home?* Discuss which homes students like the most and why.

- Explain that informative posters combine text and pictures to get people's attention. Ask: *How do the example posters combine text and pictures? Are they effective?*

- Ask students to bring an example of an informative poster to the next class. They can discuss what the posters are about and how good the design is.

↻ **Flipped classroom activity**

Step 2: Analyse the model for the project 🖱 Unit 5

Out of class: have students read the model poster and think about these questions: *What sections does the poster have? What kind of information is in each section? What order are the sections in? How do the pictures go with each section? What types of pictures does the poster use?*

In class: have students discuss their answers to the questions. Then ask them to compare the model poster with the examples brought to class.

🛡 **Learning to Learn**
Practical skills for participating in learning
Make sure students are prepared for the class discussion, and that they all take part.

Step 3: *How to* design a poster 🖱 Unit 5

- Go through the *How to* tips with the class. Ask students if the tip is related to content or design, and why it is important. Stress that both content and design are equally important in posters.

- Check that students understand that when they design their posters, they should use the ideas in this *How to* section.

Step 4: Clarify the project 🖱 Unit 5

- Follow the steps in ▸ The learning stages of project work p10 .
- Brainstorm different types of unusual traditional homes.
- Have groups discuss what resources they can use to find out information about the homes, and think about how they can present it. If they are considering a digital format, tell them to research suitable programs.

▸ My learning diary p68 **Preparation**
▸ Peer-evaluation form p69 **Preparation**

2 Development

Start this stage as soon as groups know their learning outcomes and have brainstormed different types of homes.

Step 1: Assign roles and responsibilities

- In project groups, have students decide on general roles. > Roles and responsibilities p16 Help them decide on further roles they can share, such as the ones in the diagram.

The **editor** checks that all the texts and graphics are present.

The **proofreader** checks grammar, spelling and punctuation.

The **designer** arranges the images.

The **fact checker** cross-checks content details.

The **picture manager** helps choose the images.

Step 2: Research and analyse Unit 5 p71

- Have groups start the PLAN section from **Exercise 1** and choose an unusual traditional home.

- Hand out a copy of the > Poster organiser p62 to each student.

⟳ Flipped classroom activity

Step 3: Draft and review Unit 5 p71

Out of class: have each student work on their section. Remind them to check their grammar, spelling and punctuation and to find images that support their text.

Tell students to try to include examples of language from the unit in their sections; for example, **(not) as ... as**, and **(not) + adjective + enough** for describing their home, and **have to / don't have to** for instructions on how to build it.

In class: have group members put their poster together and agree on final changes to the design. Refer them to the tips in the *How to* section.

> My learning diary p68 **Preparation**

> Peer-evaluation form p69 **Preparation**

🛡 Collaboration
Managing the sharing of tasks in a project

Monitor how group members are sharing roles and responsibilities in Steps 2 and 3. Check how well group members help each other in completing the tasks.

🔔 *Own it!* learning tip

Encouraging responsibility

Tell students it is important to complete their sections on time so that their groups can finish the project in class. Remind group members of their general roles. Discuss any problems groups may be having in keeping to schedule. Discuss why this is happening and encourage or suggest possible solutions.

3 Production

Schedule presentation times and stick to them, so that all groups can present their posters. Spread the presentations over a few classes, if necessary. Allow enough time for each presentation and for questions.

Before groups produce their final drafts, talk about how they will present their information. If they choose to present it digitally, help them to use the available classroom technology. If this is not possible, suggest other ideas, such as a walk-in display.

> Presentation ideas p19

As students complete their projects, check their abilities in the following Competencies.

Learning to Learn
Practical skills for participating in learning

Participates sensibly and positively in learning activities in class.

Evidence: Students listen actively, ask questions and express opinions in class discussions.

Understands essential grammatical terms and concepts.

Evidence: Posters have accurate examples of language from the unit.

Collaboration
Managing the sharing of tasks in a project

Ensures that work is fairly divided among members in group activities.

Evidence: Groups divide tasks according to their roles.

Offers to help others finish a task.

Evidence: Group members work together to complete their poster on time.

Step 1: Prepare Unit 5 p71

- Go through the PRESENT section in **Exercise 2**.

- As groups prepare their project, ask questions, for example: *Does your poster include photos, maps and drawings? Are you happy with the title? Are all the sections complete? Is the handwriting clear? Did you check the grammar, spelling and punctuation? Are the facts correct?* Say that each group member will present

their section. Give students time to practise in their groups. (See Differentiated instruction activities below for further practice.)

- Remind groups of the presentation date and how much time each group will have.

Differentiated instruction

Support
Help students look at their work, and each other's work. Help them to suggest ways to improve their work.
Consolidation
Encourage students to use different resources (websites, dictionaries) to check facts, language and spelling.
Extension
Let students make final decisions over corrections. Encourage them to explain their reasons to their group.

Step 2: Present Unit 5

- If the poster is digital, one group member may have the role of technician.

- Have groups present their posters. Remind students to interact with their audience and ask for questions at the end of their presentation.

- Tell the class to make notes on what they like about each poster.

Step 3: Reflect Unit 5

- Have students say what they like about each poster and why, before voting on their favourite. Then ask: *Was planning / researching / designing your poster easy / difficult? Why / Why not?*

- Encourage students to think about each stage of the project process, including positive experiences and things they could improve.

> Peer-evaluation form p69   **Production**

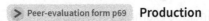 Go to the digital collaboration space to set, track and assess students' work, or allow students to share and comment on their own work.

Project evaluation rubric: a poster

Use these project-specific descriptors and your choice of descriptors from the **>** Evaluation rubric p21 to check students individually or in groups. Make your own evaluation form. **>** Teacher's evaluation form p70

	4	3	2	1
Creativity	Product is well organised with creative ideas. It has a short and interesting title. It uses borders and includes attractive photos, maps and drawings.	Product is organised with creative ideas. It has a short and fairly interesting title. It uses borders and includes some attractive photos, maps and drawings.	Product has creative ideas but lacks organisation. It has a title, but it's either too long or not interesting. It includes some attractive images, but doesn't use borders.	Product lacks creative ideas and organisation. It is missing a title. It doesn't use any design features and most images are unrelated to the topic.
Language use	Product shows excellent use of grammar, punctuation and spelling. Excellent use of language from unit. Project is understandable with only a few or no mistakes.	Product shows good use of grammar, punctuation and spelling. Good use of language from unit. Project is understandable with some mistakes.	Product shows adequate use of grammar, punctuation and spelling. Adequate use of language from unit. Project is understandable, but some sections need further explanation.	Product shows poor use of grammar, punctuation and spelling. Poor or no use of language from unit. Project is confusing and almost impossible to understand.

 Cambridge Life Competencies Framework
You can also check students' progress in the following foundation layers.

FOUNDATION LAYERS	ABILITIES	ACTIONS
Digital Literacy	• Use digital tools	finding content and cross-checking facts on various websites, using digital tools to design and present posters, sharing work online
Discipline Knowledge	• Convince the audience	explaining facts and images, demonstrating knowledge, giving details, answering questions

↻ Flipped classroom activities

Evaluate

In project groups, have students discuss their completed Peer-evaluation forms and ways to work better as a group. **>** Peer-evaluation form p69

Out of class: have students think about their progress at home. **>** My learning diary p68 **Production**

In class: discuss what students learned using the information from their learning diaries.
> My learning diary p68 **Production**

AN INFORMATION LEAFLET

- **Learning outcome:** make an information leaflet
- **Skills:** decide how the group will work together, decide on the sections and images, work individually and as a group, give feedback on first drafts
- **Resources:** two or more information leaflets, Information leaflet organiser p63, My time-management plan p71
- **Evaluation tools:** Project evaluation rubric p45, KWL chart p67, Peer-evaluation form p69, Teacher's evaluation form p70

 Student's Book pp78–79

Before you start
Collect two or three different types of leaflets to show students in class.

1 Preparation

Step 1: Introduce the topic

- Introduce the topic of information leaflets after doing the reading exercises. p72

- Show students the leaflets. Encourage them to say what they are and who they are for. Ask: *What are information leaflets? Why do people read them? What are these leaflets about?*

- Explain that leaflets use short texts to give information. For example, they tell people about an event, are used to sell something or give suggestions and advice. Have students come up with some examples.

- Ask students to bring a leaflet to the next class (preferably in English). They can discuss which leaflets they like / don't like and why.

Step 2: Analyse the model for the project 📖 pp78–79

- Complete **Exercises 1 to 3**.

  Answers **1** a **2** 2 T 3 F 4 F 5 T 6 T **3** Our bodies in the desert: thirst, heat cramps; Desert weather: sandstorms; Desert animals: snakes, scorpions

- Ask questions about the leaflet, for example: *What information is in the fact file? (Facts about deserts.) What sections can you see? What questions are there for each section? What can you see in the photos? Who is the leaflet for?*

- Revise the language from the unit. Ask students to find examples of the **zero** and **first conditional**, *should* and *must*. Ask why the leaflet uses these structures (to give suggestions and advice).

🛡 Critical Thinking
Understanding and analysing links between ideas

Use the questions in Step 2 to check how well students understand the purpose of the model leaflet and how the advice is presented.

Step 3: *How to* work in groups 📖 p78

- 🎧 6.12 Go through the three ways of working listed in **Exercise 4**. Say that in the audio, the students will talk about how they worked in their groups. Play the audio and check answers.

  Answers **4** 1 b 2 a 3 c

- In pairs, students discuss the question in **Exercise 5**.

- Check that students understand that when they work in groups, they should use the ideas in this *How to* section.

Step 4: Clarify the project 📖 pp78–79

- Follow the steps in .

- Brainstorm remote places and habitats with the class.

- Have students discuss what resources they can use for researching the brainstormed items.

> KWL chart p67 **Know and Want to know**

> Peer-evaluation form p69 **Preparation**

② Development

Start this stage as soon as groups know their learning outcomes and have discussed what resources to use.

Step 1: Assign roles and responsibilities

- In project groups, have students decide on general roles. > Roles and responsibilities p16 Help them decide on further roles they can share. Draw a diagram like this on the board:

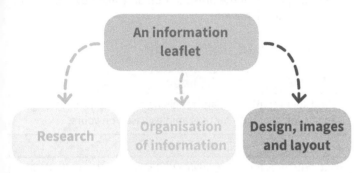

- Ask questions related to each section in the diagram. Discuss the tasks and roles required to create an information leaflet.

  Research: *Where can you find information? How can you check that the facts are correct? Who will help put together the information and suggest which is best to use?*

  Organisation of information: *What is the purpose of the leaflet? What sections will it have? What are the main and supporting ideas? How will you present the information? Who will help organise it?*

  Design, images and layout: *How will you make the leaflet look good and easy to read? Where can you find images? Who will help choose the images and decide on the layout?*

- Encourage students to take notes and decide on roles.

Step 2: Research and analyse 📖 p79 ⏱ p71

- Have groups start the PLAN section from **Exercise 6** and choose a remote place or habitat. Remind students of the three ways of working in groups from Exercise 5. Ask them to decide which way they want to work.

⟳ Flipped classroom activity

Out of class: have students write their sections, prepare their versions of the leaflets or do their tasks, depending on the way of working they have chosen.

In class: have groups complete the rest of the PLAN section. Give each group a copy of the > Information leaflet organiser p63 to help them plan their information.

Step 3: Draft and review 📖 p79 ⏱ p71

- Have groups draw up a rough plan of their leaflet. Remind them to think about the organisation of information and the design and layout discussed in Step 1.

- Allow time for drafting and reviewing. Encourage students to use the language from the unit when making suggestions or giving advice.

- Have groups share their draft with another group. Tell them to exchange opinions and suggest improvements.

- Encourage group members to improve their work out of class in line with their roles. Have them bring their ideas to the next class.

⊡ Communication
Managing conversations

Monitor progress of the tasks in Step 3 to check how well students understand each other's ideas and suggestions.

⌂ *Own it!* learning tip

Listening actively

When groups are sharing opinions about the first drafts, check that they are listening to each other's ideas and asking questions to get information or more details. Monitor to help with useful language, for example: *What do you mean? Can you repeat that? Can you explain?* Check that students show interest and respond respectfully to feedback.

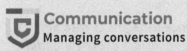 **Development**

3 Production

Schedule presentation times and stick to them. Remember that these projects will be displayed on the classroom wall. Allow enough time for students to look at all the leaflets, ask questions and give feedback.

Before groups produce their final drafts, have them decide on the format and layout of their leaflet. It could be bi-fold or tri-fold, for example. You can also give ideas for the classroom walk-in display.

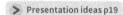 **> Presentation ideas p19**

As students complete their projects, check their abilities in the following Competencies.

Critical Thinking
Understanding and analysing links between ideas

Compares points and arguments from different sources.

Evidence: Students use their research to produce a clear leaflet.

Identifies the basic structure of an argument.

Evidence: Leaflet has a clear, logical structure with well-presented sections.

Communication
Managing conversations

Uses appropriate language to negotiate meaning: to show understanding; to signal lack of understanding; to seek clarification.

Evidence: Groups discuss different aspects of their leaflets, and ask and answer questions in order to agree on the final product.

Step 1: Prepare 📖 p79 ⏱ p71

- Go through the PRESENT section in **Exercise 7**.

- As groups prepare their project, monitor how they are working together. Remind them of the ideas in the *How to* section.

- Check the language in the leaflets, especially the use of **should** and **must** and the **zero and first conditional**. (See Differentiated instruction activities below for further practice.)

- Remind groups of the presentation date and how much time each group will have.

Differentiated instruction

Support
Help students with language for giving suggestions. Encourage them to come up with more examples based on yours.

Consolidation
Elicit structures for giving advice that students can use in their leaflets. Ask: *What are three things you should/must do?*

Extension
Have students correct each other's work and suggest more examples of structures for giving advice.

Step 2: Present 📖 p79

- For this project, students walk around and look at the leaflets on the wall. Group members can take turns standing by their display to answer questions.

- Draw attention to the CHECK section in **Exercise 8**. Tell groups to ask each other about how they worked together. Encourage them to discuss what went well.

- Have group members present their leaflets to the rest of the class.

- Help students interact with one another and presenters respond appropriately to their classmates' ideas.

Step 3: Reflect 📖 p79

- After the presentations, hold a class discussion on the CHECK questions in **Exercise 8**.

- Encourage students to think about each stage of the project process, including positive experiences and things they could improve.

> Peer-evaluation form p69 **Production**

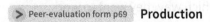 🖱 Go to the digital collaboration space to set, track and assess students' work, or allow students to share and comment on their own work.

Project evaluation rubric: an information leaflet

Use these project-specific descriptors and your choice of descriptors from the > Evaluation rubric p21 to check students individually or in groups. Make your own evaluation form. > Teacher's evaluation form p70

	4	3	2	1
Creativity	Product has a very original and attractive design. It uses many interesting images and is divided into clear sections. It includes a lot of interesting facts. All group members contributed creatively.	Product has an original and attractive design. It uses some interesting images and is divided into fairly clear sections. It includes some interesting facts. Most group members contributed creatively.	Product has a clear design that largely follows the model. It uses images and is divided into sections, though these are not always clear. It includes very few interesting facts. Only some group members contributed creatively.	Product has an unattractive design with little creativity and it doesn't follow the model. It doesn't use images and there are no clear sections. It doesn't include any interesting facts. Members didn't work as a group and there was little creativity.
Language use	Excellent use of language from unit (*should, must,* zero and first conditional). Project is understandable with only a few mistakes.	Good use of language from unit (*should, must,* zero and first conditional). Project is understandable with some mistakes.	Adequate use of language from unit (*should, must,* zero and first conditional). Project is understandable, but some sections need further explanation.	Poor or no use of language from unit (*should, must,* zero and first conditional). Project is confusing and almost impossible to understand.

 Cambridge Life Competencies Framework
You can also check students' progress in the following foundation layers.

FOUNDATION LAYERS	ABILITIES	ACTIONS
Emotional Development and Wellbeing	• Empathise and build relationships	sharing roles, making decisions together, checking understanding, reflecting on strengths and weaknesses, giving advice on how to improve
Discipline Knowledge	• Convince the audience	explaining facts and images, summarising information, giving details and advice about the topic, answering questions

↻ Flipped classroom activities

Evaluate
In project groups, have students discuss their completed Peer-evaluation forms and ways to work better as a group. > Peer-evaluation form p69

Out of class: have students think about their progress at home. > KWL chart p67 Learned

In class: discuss what students learned, using the information from their KWL charts. > KWL chart p67 Learned

A 3D ROOM PLAN

- **Learning outcome:** design a 3D room plan
- **Skills:** draw a diagram (digitally or on paper), decide what technology to include, invent a new technological device, describe the items in the room plan by using call-out boxes
- **Resources:** two or more room plans, Room plan organiser p64, My time-management plan p71
- **Evaluation tools:** Project evaluation rubric p49, My learning diary p68, Peer-evaluation form p69, Teacher's evaluation form p70

 Unit 7

Before you start
Collect two or three examples of room plans to show students in class. Use the internet or other real room plans you may have access to, such as the school's.

1 Preparation

Step 1: Introduce the topic

- Introduce the topic of room plans after doing the vocabulary exercises 📖 p83, and after students have talked about different technological devices. Alternatively, wait until *will, may* and *might* have been practised. 📖 p87

- Show students the room plans. Ask: *What are these? What do they show? Who creates room plans? What are they for?* You can have students draw a room plan of the classroom, including fixed objects, such as doors and windows, and other furniture.

- Explain that a 3D room plan is a diagram of a room or rooms in a building that shows the view from above. Say that it can include measurements, fixed objects, furniture and sometimes electric systems and water pipes.

- Ask students to find an example of a room plan online and bring it to the next class. It can show one or more rooms in a building. Students can describe the room plans in groups.

Step 2: Analyse the model for the project Unit 7

- Have students describe the model room plan. Ask: *What furniture does the classroom have? How is it different from our classroom?* Students read the texts.

- Ask further questions, for example: *Which ideas do you like? Would you like these things in your classroom?* Discuss how classrooms will be different in the future. (See Differentiated instruction activities below for further practice.)

Differentiated instruction

Support
Have students find examples of predictions in the texts. They can discuss which predictions are most likely to come true.

Consolidation
In pairs, have students take turns to read a prediction from one of the texts and guess the item it refers to.

Extension
Have students work in pairs. They cover the texts and take turns to point to an item in the room plan and make a prediction about what it will do.

Step 3: *How to* design a room plan 🖱 Unit 7

- Go through the *How to* tips with the class. Different students say why each idea is important.

- Help students understand that when they design their room plans, they should use the ideas in this *How to* section.

🛡 Critical Thinking
Evaluating ideas, arguments and options
Encourage students to think about problems they might have as they follow the *How to* tips. Have them discuss possible solutions.

Step 4: Clarify the project 🖱 Unit 7

- Follow the steps in ❯ The learning stages of project work p10 .

- Brainstorm different rooms for students to choose from. These can be real or imaginary places.

❯ My learning diary p68 **Preparation**

❯ Peer-evaluation form p69 **Preparation**

2 Development

Start this stage as soon as groups know their learning outcomes and have brainstormed different rooms to choose from.

Step 1: Assign roles and responsibilities

- In project groups, have students decide on general roles. > Roles and responsibilities p16 Help them decide on further roles they can share, such as the ones in the diagram.

The **architect** measures and helps draw the plans.

The **writer** helps describe the room's features.

The **researcher** helps find information about the room and building.

The **interior designer** suggests what furniture to include.

The **technological expert** makes suggestions for modern technology and the new invention.

Step 2: Research and analyse Unit 7 p71

- Have groups start the PLAN section from **Exercise 1**. Tell them to choose a room and brainstorm modern technology.

- Have groups draw an outline of their room. Draw attention to the model room plan notes. Ask students to plan their room making similar notes on technological devices, what they do and where they go, as well as their new invention and other furniture.

- Ask groups to decide on their room plan format: either print or digital. Encourage those who have chosen a digital format to look for free programs online.

- Hand out a copy of the > Room plan organiser p64 to each student. Tell students to copy a drawing of their room plan in the first part, with all the items their groups agreed on.

- Have group members decide who will prepare which texts for each of the items.

🔔 *Own it!* learning tip

Disagreeing appropriately

If students cannot agree on some of the items to include in their room plans, encourage polite discussion and allow them to give their opinions explaining their reasons. Have them make alternative suggestions to come to a solution everyone is happy with. Monitor to help with useful language, for example: *I'm not sure about … I don't agree because … Why don't we … ? How about … ? Maybe we should …*

🔄 **Flipped classroom activity**

Step 3: Draft and review 🖈 Unit 7 🕓 p71

Out of class: group members prepare their sections, making notes in the second part of their organisers. Remind them to use language from the unit: **will** for predictions and the **infinitive of purpose**.

In class: group members check each other's work, paying attention to spelling and grammar.

Groups put together a final version of their room plan. If groups are creating it digitally, they may need to do this out of class.

🛡 **Collaboration**
Working towards a resolution related to a task

Monitor students' ability to agree on things and make changes to the final plan as they listen to each other's ideas.

> My learning diary p68 **Development**

> Peer-evaluation form p69 **Development**

3 Production

Schedule presentation times and stick to them, so that all groups can present their room plans. Spread the presentations over a few classes, if necessary. Allow enough time for each presentation and for questions.

Before groups produce their final drafts, offer help and suggest ideas for them to complete their digital or print room plans successfully.

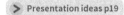 **Presentation ideas p19**

As students complete their projects, check their abilities in the following Competencies.

Critical Thinking
Evaluating ideas, arguments and options

Examines possible solutions to a given problem and states how effective they are.

Evidence: Groups make new versions of their work when necessary and share opinions about new ideas.

Assesses strengths and weaknesses of possible solutions.

Evidence: Groups make decisions in order to achieve the learning outcomes.

Collaboration
Working towards a resolution related to a task

Is aware when others have divergent views and ideas for solving a problem or task.

Evidence: Students listen carefully to each other's opinions and make decisions together.

Is able to propose solutions that include other views and ideas to own.

Evidence: Students decide what to include, considering all group members' ideas.

Step 1: Prepare Unit 7 🕐 p71

- Go through the PRESENT section from **Exercise 2**. Say that each group member will present their section.

- Allow time for groups to finish their room plans. If they disagree, remind them to do so politely.

- Monitor to check that the room plans have a clear design, the text in the call-out boxes is clear, and the boxes correctly match the items in the diagram.

- Ask students to check spelling and grammar. Help with corrections as necessary.

Step 2: Present Unit 7

- Draw attention to the CHECK section in **Exercise 3**. Ask the class to think about these questions as they listen to each other's presentations.

- Remind speakers to look at their audience, speak slowly and clearly, and smile. Tell them to point to the section of the room plan they describe. If students are presenting digitally, they can zoom in on specific features.

- Have groups present their room plans.

- Tell the class to make notes on what they like about each room plan and new invention.

Step 3: Reflect 🖱 Unit 7

- After all the presentations, hold a class discussion on the CHECK questions in **Exercise 3**.

- Have the class discuss what they like about each room plan and invention and why. Ask: *What have you learned about room plans? What makes a good room plan? What were the most interesting technological devices?*

- Encourage students to think about each stage of the project process, including positive experiences and things they could improve.

> **Peer-evaluation form p69** **Production**

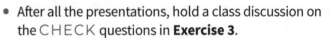 Go to the digital collaboration space to set, track and assess students' work, or allow students to share and comment on their own work.

Project evaluation rubric: a 3D room plan

Use these project-specific descriptors and your choice of descriptors from the `> Evaluation rubric p21` to check students individually or in groups. Make your own evaluation form. `> Teacher's evaluation form p70`

	4	3	2	1
Creativity	Product has a very attractive design with clear labels. Its call-out boxes show many creative ideas. It presents a new invention with a clear description of its purpose and advantages.	Product has an attractive design with clear labels. Its call-out boxes show some creative ideas. It presents a new invention with a fairly clear description of its purpose and advantages.	Product has an adequate design with mostly clear labels. Its call-out boxes show only one or two creative ideas. It presents a new invention, but its purpose or advantages are unclear.	Product has an unclear design and is either missing most labels, or these are unclear. It doesn't have call-out boxes, or these don't show any creative ideas. It doesn't present a new invention.
Language use	Excellent use of language from unit (*will*; infinitive of purpose). Project is understandable with only a few mistakes.	Good use of language from unit (*will*; infinitive of purpose). Project is understandable with some mistakes.	Adequate use of language from unit (*will*; infinitive of purpose). Project is understandable, but some sections need further explanation.	Poor or no use of language from unit (*will*; infinitive of purpose). Project is confusing and poorly written.

Cambridge Life Competencies Framework

You can also check students' progress in the following foundation layers.

FOUNDATION LAYERS	ABILITIES	ACTIONS
Discipline Knowledge	• Use digital tools	finding content on various websites, creating documents, sharing work online, using digital room plan programs
Emotional Development and Wellbeing	• Manage emotions	reflecting on strengths and weaknesses, verbalising emotions and disagreeing appropriately, finding solutions

⟳ Flipped classroom activities

Evaluate

In project groups, have students discuss their completed Peer-evaluation forms and ways to work better as a group. `> Peer-evaluation form p69`

Out of class: have students think about their progress at home. `> My learning diary p68` **Production**

In class: discuss what students learned using the information from their learning diaries. `> My learning diary p68` **Production**

A TIMELINE

- **Learning outcome:** make a timeline
- **Skills:** research information and images; manage time: prioritise tasks, set long- and short-term deadlines, divide up tasks
- **Resources:** two or more timelines, Timeline organiser p65, My time-management plan p71
- **Evaluation tools:** Project evaluation rubric p53, KWL chart p67, Peer-evaluation form p69, Teacher's evaluation form p70

📖 Student's Book pp102–103

Before you start
Find two or more timelines about inventions or events from magazines or the internet to show students in class.

1 Preparation

Step 1: Introduce the topic

- Introduce the topic of timelines after doing the grammar exercises. 📖 p97

- Show students the timelines. Ask: *What can timelines be about? What information do these timelines have? How do they present it?*

- Explain that timelines are lines that show a sequence of events in chronological order. Say that a timeline helps you understand when things happened and in what order. Point out that many timelines have images to help describe events.

- Ask students to bring an example of a timeline to the next class. They can say where they found the timelines (newspapers, magazines, online) and discuss what they are about. Then they can compare the designs.

Step 2: Analyse the model for the project 📖 pp102–103

- Complete **Exercises 1 and 2**.

    Answers 1 1 C 2 B 3 D 4 E 5 A 6 F 2 2 b 3 a, c 4 f 5 b, d, f 6 e, f

- Ask questions about the content and design of the model timeline, for example: *What is the purpose of this timeline? What is its shape? How do the design and shape relate to the theme? Is the timeline easy to follow?*

- Revise the language from the unit. Ask students to find examples of the **present perfect for experience** and **reflexive and indefinite pronouns**.

Step 3: *How to* **manage your time** 📖 p102

- Go through the ideas in **Exercise 3** with the class. Students take turns to call out the answers.

    Answers 3 b, c, d, f, g, h

- As you discuss students' answers, ask questions to check comprehension: *Why is it important to prioritise tasks? What is a short- / long-term deadline?*

- 🎧 8.12 Play the audio and check answers.

    Answers 4 b, c, d, f, g

- Help students understand that when they have to manage their time for the project, they should use the ideas in this *How to* section.

> 🛡 **Learning to Learn**
> **Practical skills for participating in learning**
> Have students think about time-management problems they have had in past project work. Ask them to come up with another idea for effective time management.

Step 4: Clarify the project 📖 pp102–103

- Follow the steps in  > The learning stages of project work p10 .

- Have groups brainstorm possible themes for their timeline. Tell them to bring a list with their ideas to the next class.

> KWL chart p67   **Know and Want to know**

> Peer-evaluation form p69   **Preparation**

② Development

Start this stage as soon as groups know their learning outcomes and have a list of possible themes for their timelines.

Step 1: Assign roles and responsibilities

- In project groups, have students decide on general roles. > Roles and responsibilities p16 Help them decide on further roles they can share. Draw a diagram like this on the board:

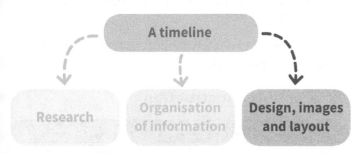

- Ask questions related to each section in the diagram. Discuss the tasks and roles required to create a timeline.

  Research: *Where can you find information? How can you check facts, dates and events? Who will help put all the information together and suggest which is best to use?*

  Organisation of information: *How will you decide on the key dates and events? What facts do you need next to each date? Who will help organise the information?*

  Design, images and layout: *What shape will your timeline have? How will you make your timeline attractive and easy to read? Where can you find images? Who will help choose the images and decide on the layout?*

- Encourage students to take notes and decide on roles.

Step 2: Research and analyse 📖 p103 ⏰ p71

- Have groups start the P L A N section from **Exercise 5**. Tell them to choose a theme.

- Refer students to the diagram for tasks and roles from Step 1. Have groups discuss what tasks they need to do to complete their timeline. If necessary, play Track 8.12 again for ideas.

- Give students a long-term deadline for the whole project, and let them set short-term deadlines for the tasks they discussed.

- Remind students also to use > My time-management plan p71 .

🕐 Flipped classroom activity

Out of class: have students research information and images for their timelines. Tell them to bring their findings to the next class.

In class: have groups check their findings together and decide which information and images to use.

Step 3: Draft and review 📖 p103 ⏰ p71

- Hand out a copy of the > Timeline organiser p65 to each group.

- Have groups use the organiser to put together the key information and ideas for images. Encourage students to think of attractive and imaginative ways to present their timeline.

- Go through the P L A N section and help groups to make sure that their timelines include all the items mentioned.

- Have groups write and edit their timelines, if possible including examples of the **present perfect for experiences** and **reflexive and indefinite pronouns**.

- As groups review their projects, remind them of the time-management ideas in the *How to* section.

🛡️ Creative Thinking
Creating new content from own ideas or other resources

Monitor groups' understanding of the events in their timelines, as well as their creativity when presenting this sequence.

> Peer-evaluation form p69 **Development**

3 Production

Schedule presentation times and stick to them. Remember that these projects will be displayed on the classroom wall. Allow enough time for students to look at all the timelines, ask questions and give feedback.

As groups work on their final drafts, give them tips on how best to present their timelines with images. Tell students they can follow the steps for making a storyboard. Alternatively, groups could choose to make their timelines digitally, using a free online timeline maker.

> Presentation ideas p19

As students complete their projects, check their abilities in the following Competencies.

 Learning to Learn
Practical skills for participating in learning

Uses metacognitive strategies (e.g. time management) to maximise learning.

Evidence: Groups share tasks and follow the ideas in the *How to* section.

Takes effective notes in class and from homework reading.

Evidence: Group members research and choose the key facts about their theme.

 Creative Thinking
Creating new content from own ideas or other resources

Writes or tells an original story, given prompts or without prompts.

Evidence: Timeline describes events in chronological order with pictures.

Responds imaginatively to contemporary or historical events and ideas.

Evidence: Timeline presents information in an imaginative way.

Step 1: Prepare 📖 p103 ⏱ p71

- Go through the checklist in the PLAN section from **Exercise 5** again.

- As groups prepare their project, ask questions, for example: *How did you decide on the design? Have you included all the key dates, people and events? Do the images match the texts? Are you sharing and completing tasks on time?*

- Point to **Exercise 6** in the PRESENT section. Remind groups of the presentation date.

Step 2: Present 📖 p103

- For this project, students walk around and look at the timelines on the wall. Group members can take turns standing by their display to answer questions.

- Draw attention to the CHECK section from **Exercise 7**. Tell the class to think about the question as they look at each other's timelines. Have them write down interesting facts.

- Have group members present their timelines. (See Differentiated instruction activities below for further practice.)

- Help students to work with one another, asking and answering questions.

Differentiated instruction

Support
Have groups cut up their timeline organisers into six sections, shuffle them, and pass them to another group to reorder.
Consolidation
Ask students questions about other groups' timelines and have them find out the answers.
Extension
In project groups, students write questions about their timelines. Then pairs of groups quiz each other.

Step 3: Reflect 📖 p103

- After the presentations, ask the class to vote for their favourite timelines, and to say which ones have interesting facts.

- Encourage students to think about each stage of the project process, including positive experiences and things they could improve.

🔔 *Own it!* learning tip

Sharing tasks

As groups discuss the projects in Step 3, remind them of the time-management ideas in the *How to* section. Ask if everyone could complete their task. Find out what groups did if any part of the project became difficult.

> Peer-evaluation form p69   **Production**

🔗 Go to the digital collaboration space to set, track and assess students' work, or allow students to share and comment on their own work.

Project evaluation rubric: a timeline

Use these project-specific descriptors and your choice of descriptors from the `> Evaluation rubric p21` to check students individually or in groups. Make your own evaluation form. `> Teacher's evaluation form p70`

	4	3	2	1
Creativity	Product is clear and logical, with an original design that relates to the theme. It uses a wide variety of images that clearly illustrate the events. It includes a wide range of interesting facts.	Product is mostly clear and logical, with an original design that relates to the theme. It uses a variety of images that illustrate the events quite well. It includes mostly interesting facts.	Product is clear and logical only in parts. It has a good design, but is only loosely related to the theme. It uses images that only illustrate some of the events. It includes facts, but only a few are interesting.	Product is unclear and illogical, with a design that is not related to the theme. It uses very few or no images, and these don't illustrate the events well. It doesn't include any interesting facts.
Language use	Excellent use of language from unit (present perfect for experiences; reflexive and indefinite pronouns). Project is understandable with only a few mistakes.	Good use of language from unit (present perfect for experiences; reflexive and indefinite pronouns). Project is understandable with some mistakes.	Adequate use of language from unit (present perfect for experiences; reflexive and indefinite pronouns). Project is understandable, but some sections need further explanation.	Poor or no use of language from unit (present perfect for experiences; reflexive and indefinite pronouns). Project is confusing and almost impossible to understand.

Cambridge Life Competencies Framework

You can also check students' progress in the following foundation layers.

FOUNDATION LAYERS	ABILITIES	ACTIONS
Emotional Development and Wellbeing	• Empathise and build relationships	sharing and prioritising tasks, agreeing on and trying to stick to deadlines, giving constructive feedback
Discipline Knowledge	• Convince the audience	giving facts and details, arranging information in the correct order, presenting in a clear and logical manner (written and oral), answering questions

○ Flipped classroom activities

Evaluate

In project groups, have students discuss their completed Peer-evaluation forms and ways to work better as a group. `> Peer-evaluation form p69`

Out of class: have students think about their progress at home. `> KWL chart p67` **Learned**

In class: discuss what students learned, using the information from their KWL charts. `> KWL chart p67` **Learned**

9 THE CULTURE PROJECT

A WEBPAGE

- **Learning outcome:** make a webpage about a music festival

- **Skills:** research information and use a spidergram to organise it, research images and maps, use a webpage template

- **Resources:** two or more webpages about music festivals, Webpage organiser p66, My time-management plan p71

- **Evaluation tools:** Project evaluation rubric p57, My learning diary p68, Peer-evaluation form p69, Teacher's evaluation form p70

 Unit 9

Before you start
Research festivals from around the world. Choose two or three and find webpages about them to show students in class.

1 Preparation

Step 1: Introduce the topic

- Introduce the topic of webpages after doing the reading exercises. 📖 p108 Draw attention to the events in the guide. Ask: *Where can we find out about arts and entertainment events?*

- Show students the webpages. Ask: *What are they about? What information is in each section? Is there any information missing? Who are the webpages for? Would you like to go to these festivals? Why / Why not?*

- Ask students which webpages they visit and what for. Ask: *Do you visit webpages about festivals?*

- Ask students to bring an example of a webpage about a festival to the next class. They can discuss the webpages in groups.

Step 2: Analyse the model for the project  Unit 9

- Have students look at the sections, titles and pictures on the model webpage. Ask: *What is this webpage about? Who might read it?* Then students read the webpage.

- Ask: *Where is this festival? Who goes to it? Where is flamenco part of the culture? What can visitors do? Where can they stay? Have you been to this festival? Would you like to go? Why / Why not?*

- Ask questions about the webpage's design and purpose: *Does it look good? What is it used for?* (See Differentiated instruction activities below for further practice.)

Differentiated instruction

Support
In pairs, have students make true/false sentences about the webpage to test another pair.
Consolidation
Have students make a list of other possible events at the festival that the webpage doesn't mention. Have them agree on the best events.
Extension
Tell students to imagine they are going to the Jerez Festival. Have them plan three things they are going to do.

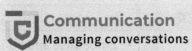 Communication
Managing conversations

Help students take part in discussions while using appropriate language for each task.

Step 3: *How to* design a webpage 👆 Unit 9

- Ask students: *Have you ever thought about designing a webpage?* Then go through the *How to* tips with the class.

- Draw attention to *what a visitor will want to know* in the third tip. Explain that a webpage should have a clear purpose.

- Check students understand that when they design their webpages, they should use the ideas in this *How to* section.

Step 4: Clarify the project 👆 Unit 9

- Follow the steps in > The learning stages of project work p10 .

- Brainstorm festivals from around the world that students may know about. Have groups discuss where they can find out more information.

> My learning diary p68 **Preparation**

> Peer-evaluation form p69 **Preparation**

② Development

Start this stage as soon as groups know their learning outcomes and have discussed what sources to use.

Step 1: Assign roles and responsibilities

- In project groups, have students decide on general roles.
  > Roles and responsibilities p16 Help them decide on further roles they can share, such as the ones in the diagram.

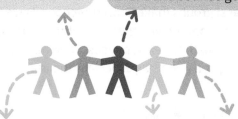

The **events organiser** helps describe events and activities.

The **marketing manager** makes sure the webpage looks and sounds good.

The **tourist information officer** helps provide information on where to stay and how to get there.

The **web designer** helps create the webpage.

The **editor** makes sure texts and images fit in each section.

Step 2: Research and analyse Unit 9 p71

- Have groups start the PLAN section from **Exercise 1**. Have them decide on their festival.

- Have groups make notes about their festival. Hand out a copy of the > Webpage organiser p66 to each student. Students use the spidergram to plan their notes.

⟳ Flipped classroom activity

Out of class: have students research interesting historical facts and think of imaginative activities. They can add the information to their spidergrams.

Have students refer to the example webpage designs in the second part of their organisers. Encourage them to look for other online templates and draw a webpage design in the space provided.

In class: have groups organise all the information. Then have them agree on who will prepare each section.

🔔 *Own it!* learning tip

Sharing resources

Make sure students share useful information that they have found. This can include online templates, photos, maps, drawings and facts about their festival. Ask them to encourage each other to say how they found the information.

⟳ Flipped classroom activity

Step 3: Draft and review Unit 9 p71

Out of class: have group members prepare their parts as explained in the PLAN section.

Encourage students to check the facts about their festivals in their sources.

In class: group members check each other's sections. If they haven't done so yet, groups decide on final design and content.

Out of class: led by the web designer, have groups work on the design and share and check their work online. Remind them to use a template that matches their chosen design.

🛡 Social Responsibilities
Understanding and describing own and others' cultures

Encourage students to look for cultural information about their festivals and include it in their webpages.
Ask: *How is culture important to the festival? (Use of traditional music/food/clothes, etc.)*

> My learning diary p68 **Development**
> Peer-evaluation form p69 **Development**

3 Production

Schedule presentation times and stick to them, allowing, if possible, all groups to present their webpage on a big screen. Spread the presentations over a few classes, if necessary. Allow enough time for each presentation and for questions.

Before groups produce their final webpages, help them follow the online steps for the template they have chosen to complete their project.

As students complete their projects, check their abilities in the following Competencies.

Communication
Managing conversations

Uses appropriate language to negotiate meaning: to check own understanding; to check interlocutors' understanding.

Evidence: Students make corrections based on each other's feedback.

Invites contributions from interlocutors in a conversation.

Evidence: Group members ask each other questions about their sections.

Social Responsibilities
Understanding and describing own and others' cultures

Makes informed comparisons between their own society and other societies.

Evidence: Website includes cultural observations.

Understands the contributions of different cultures to their own lives.

Evidence: Students think about the cultural importance of their festival and reasons why it's important for them.

Step 1: Prepare ☞ Unit 9 ⏰ p71

- Go through the PRESENT section in **Exercise 2**.
- As groups prepare their project, remind them of the tasks they need to complete by asking them questions. Tell them that they should be ready to answer questions, particularly about their own sections.

↻ Flipped classroom activity

Out of class: groups finish their webpages by sharing tasks online. Remind them to follow the ideas in the *How to* section.

In class: groups make final corrections. Have them focus on content: whether the webpage includes all the information a visitor needs. Then have them check spelling and grammar, especially the use of tenses.

Step 2: Present ☞ Unit 9

- Draw attention to the CHECK section from **Exercise 3**. Ask the class to think about these questions as they look at each other's webpages.
- If possible, have groups project their webpages on a big screen. Make sure each group member presents their section.
- After the presentations, students could try and use the webpages: they could click on the different features, zoom in, etc.
- Encourage students to ask questions and make notes about what they like.

Step 3: Reflect ☞ Unit 9

- After the presentations, hold a class discussion on the CHECK questions in **Exercise 3**.
- Have the class say what they like about each webpage and why. Then ask: *Which festivals would you like to go to? Why?* Finally, the class can vote on the best webpage.
- Encourage students to think about each stage of the project process, including positive experiences and things they could improve.

> Peer-evaluation form p69 **Production**

☞ Go to the digital collaboration space to set, track and assess students' work, or allow students to share and comment on their own work.

Project evaluation rubric: a webpage

Use these project-specific descriptors and your choice of descriptors from the > Evaluation rubric p21 to check students individually or in groups. Make your own evaluation form. > Teacher's evaluation form p70

	4	3	2	1
Creativity	Product's name is very interesting. Product is attractive and contains pictures for each description. It is easy to use and understand. It contains very interesting cultural information.	Product's name is interesting. Product is attractive and contains pictures for most descriptions. It is generally easy to use and understand. It contains some interesting cultural information.	Product's name is clear, but not interesting. Only some parts are attractive, and a few descriptions don't have pictures. Some parts are difficult to use or understand. It contains cultural information, but is not very interesting.	Product's name is not interesting or clear. Product is unattractive with very few pictures. It is impossible to use or understand. It doesn't contain any cultural information.
Language use	Excellent use of language from unit (future tenses). Project is understandable with only a few mistakes.	Good use of language from unit (future tenses). Project is understandable with some mistakes.	Adequate use of language from unit (future tenses). Project is understandable, but some sections need further explanation.	Poor or no use of language from unit (future tenses). Project is confusing and poorly written.

Cambridge Life Competencies Framework

You can also check students' progress in the following foundation layers.

FOUNDATION LAYERS	ABILITIES	ACTIONS
Digital Literacy	• Use digital tools	finding content, creating a webpage, sharing work online, using digital presentation techniques, adding interactive features
Discipline Knowledge	• Convince the audience	explaining facts and images, giving details, describing events, answering questions

○ Flipped classroom activities

Evaluate

In project groups, have students discuss their completed Peer-evaluation forms and ways to work better as a group. > Peer-evaluation form p69

Out of class: have students think about their progress at home. > My learning diary p68 Production

In class: discuss what students learned using the information from their learning diaries.
> My learning diary p68 Production

STORYBOARD ORGANISER

Scene 1	Scene 2	Scene 3
Script: Music: Special effects:	Script: Music: Special effects:	Script: Music: Special effects:
Scene 4	Scene 5	Scene 6
Script: Music: Special effects:	Script: Music: Special effects:	Script: Music: Special effects:
Scene 7	Scene 8	Scene 9
Script: Music: Special effects:	Script: Music: Special effects:	Script: Music: Special effects:

MUSEUM DISPLAY ORGANISER

Name of object	
Location	
Materials	
How did people make it?	
What did people use it for?	
Other interesting facts	

Write ideas for photos and pictures. You can also write the sources here.

Organise your group's display. Draw a picture.

© Cambridge University Press 2020 Unit 2 Museum display organiser

COMIC STRIP ORGANISER

© Cambridge University Press 2020 Unit 3 Comic strip organiser **PHOTOCOPIABLE**

POSTER ORGANISER

Title

Introduction (messages to attract volunteers)

Ideas for images

What?

Why?

Where?

Who?

What are the benefits?

When?

POSTER ORGANISER: A SPIDERGRAM

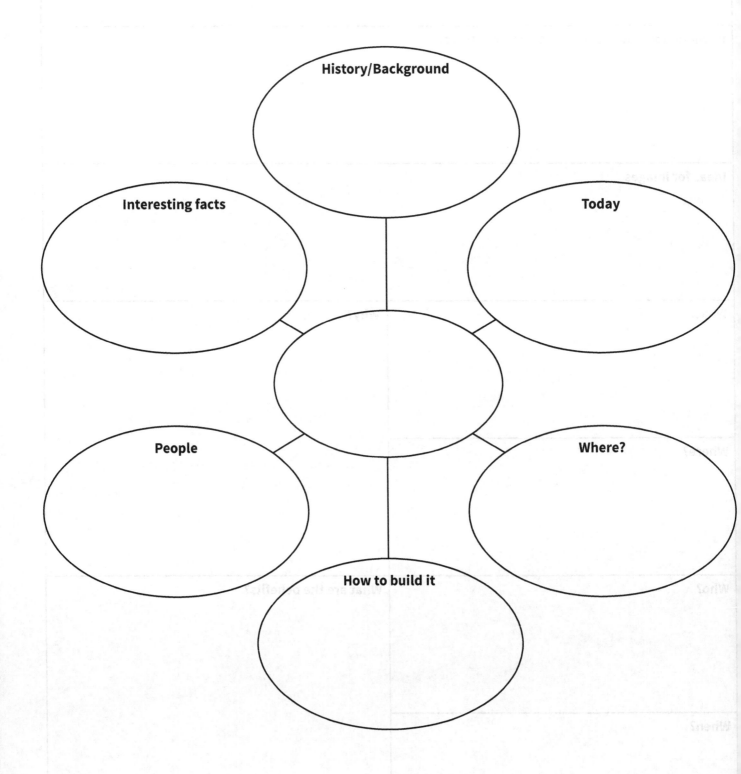

INFORMATION LEAFLET ORGANISER

Place or habitat: _____

Fact file:

Sections (e.g. weather, animals, dangers, etc.)

Image ideas:

Image ideas:

Image ideas:

Image ideas:

© Cambridge University Press 2020 Unit 6 Information leaflet organiser

ROOM PLAN ORGANISER

Items' names

What is each item for?

What will each item do?

What will we be able to do with each of the items?

NEW INVENTION! What's its name? What will it do?

TIMELINE ORGANISER

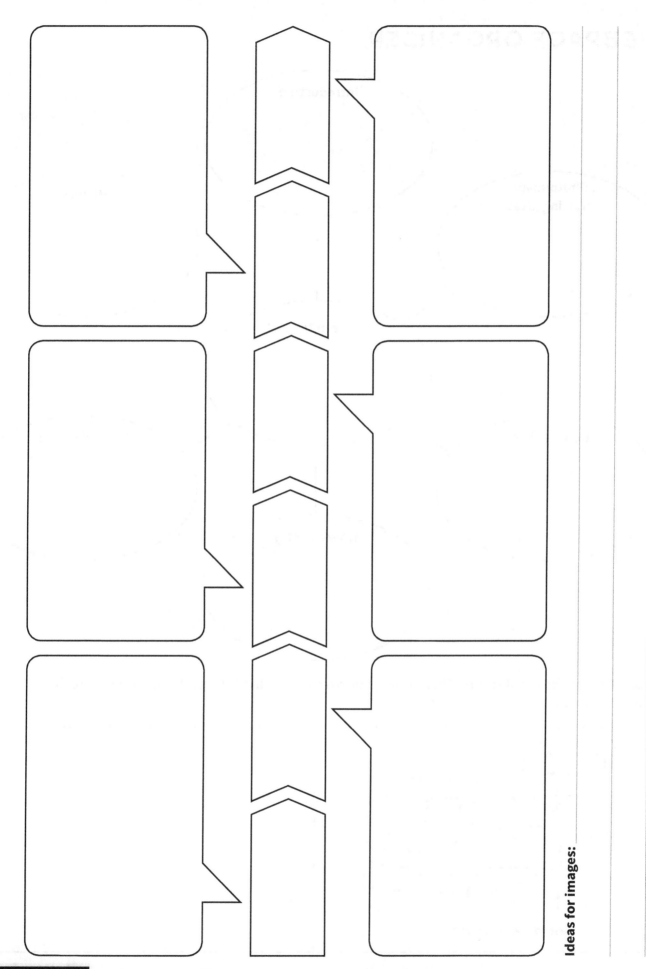

Ideas for images:

© Cambridge University Press 2020 Unit 8 Timeline organiser

WEBPAGE ORGANISER

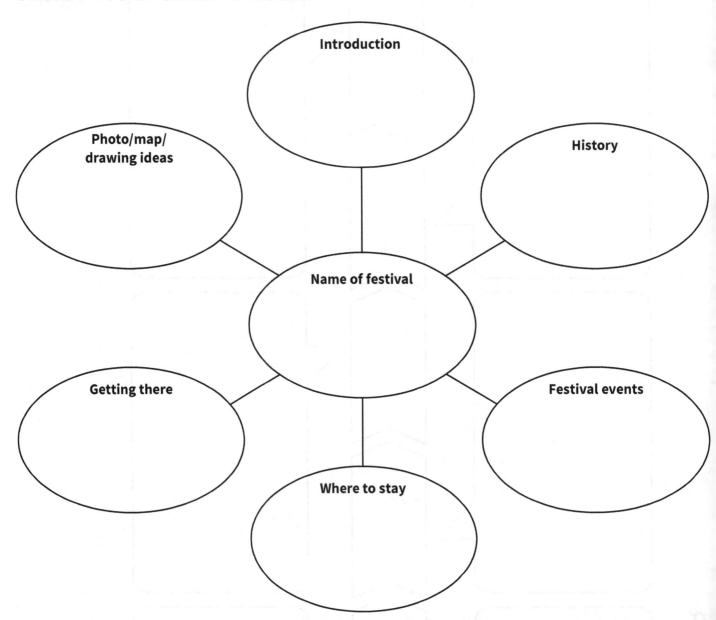

- Introduction
- Photo/map/drawing ideas
- History
- Name of festival
- Getting there
- Festival events
- Where to stay

Look at the webpage designs. Then draw your own design including all the information in your spidergram.

Name: _____

Date: _____

Unit, topic and project: _____

KWL CHART

Know	Want to know	Learned (Know now)
What do we know about the topic?	*What do we want to know about the topic?*	*What do we know now about the topic?*
		What do we know now about the tasks?
What are our tasks?		*What can we do now as a group?*

© Cambridge University Press 2020 Evaluation tools: KWL chart

Name: _____

Date: _____

Unit, topic and project: _____

MY LEARNING DIARY

1 PREPARATION
- What am I learning?   • What can I use? (for example, the internet, the library, magazines …)
- Who is in my project group?   • What is my role in the group?

2 DEVELOPMENT
- What is difficult about this project?   • Who or what can help me?   • What do I like / don't I like?
- How can we make our work better?

3 PRODUCTION
- Is it a good presentation? Why / Why not?   • In the presentation, what is my role?
- How do I feel when I give a presentation?

Name: _____

Date: _____

Unit, topic and project: _____

PEER-EVALUATION FORM

1 In your group, think about your performance. Mark (✓) the columns.

1 PREPARATION	☺	😐	☹
We listen to the instructions.			
We understand the project.			

2 DEVELOPMENT	☺	😐	☹
We do our best in the project.			
We work well as a group.			

3 PRODUCTION	☺	😐	☹
We answer questions about our work.			
We ask questions about others' work.			

2 Write one good thing about this project.

_____

_____

_____

_____

3 How can your group work better in the next project? Write one idea.

_____

_____

_____

_____

Name: _____

Date: _____

Unit, topic and project: _____

TEACHER'S EVALUATION FORM

Group or individual performance grades for the selected ✓ general areas.
Grades are as follows: 4 = Exceeds expectations, 3 = Very good, 2 = Good, 1 = Needs improvement.

✓	Areas / Outcomes	Grade	✓	Areas / Outcomes	Grade
	Learning outcomes			Creativity	
	Planning and organisation			Problem-solving skills	
	Use of information and resources			Language use	
	Collaboration (Teamwork)			Presentation skills	
	Time management			Final product	

Group or individual performance grades for the project-specific areas.
Grades are as follows: 4 = Exceeds expectations, 3 = Very good, 2 = Good, 1 = Needs improvement.

Project-specific area	Grade
1	
2	
3	
4	
5	

Cambridge Life Competencies Framework

[Student's name / Group] _____ showed (✓) did not show (✗)
development in the following competencies and skills during this project.

Competency 1	✓ / ✗	Foundation layers	✓ / ✗
		Emotional Development and Wellbeing	
		Digital Literacy	
Competency 2	✓ / ✗	Discipline Knowledge	
		Comments:	
Comments:			

Overall grade: _____

General comments:

Area(s) of improvement:

Name: _____

Date: _____

Unit, topic and project: _____

MY TIME-MANAGEMENT PLAN

**What tasks do you need to do for each step? Write them below and write the time prediction.
Then tick (✓) each task as you complete it and write the actual time it takes.**

Research and analyse

What do I need to do?	Time prediction	Actual time
1 ☐ _____	→ 🕐 _____	→ 🕐 _____
2 ☐ _____	→ 🕐 _____	→ 🕐 _____
3 ☐ _____	→ 🕐 _____	→ 🕐 _____

Draft and review

What do I need to do?	Time prediction	Actual time
1 ☐ _____	→ 🕐 _____	→ 🕐 _____
2 ☐ _____	→ 🕐 _____	→ 🕐 _____
3 ☐ _____	→ 🕐 _____	→ 🕐 _____

Prepare

What do I need to do?	Time prediction	Actual time
1 ☐ _____	→ 🕐 _____	→ 🕐 _____
2 ☐ _____	→ 🕐 _____	→ 🕐 _____
3 ☐ _____	→ 🕐 _____	→ 🕐 _____

Reflect

Answer the questions.

- I manage my time well during my project work.   ☐ Yes.   ☐ Can be better.
- I have time to complete self-evaluation tools for each stage.   ☐ Yes.   ☐ No.
- How can I improve my time management in the next project?

_____

_____

_____

 © Cambridge University Press 2020 Evaluation tools: My time-management plan

Acknowledgements

The authors and publishers acknowledge the following sources of copyright material and are grateful for the permissions granted. While every effort has been made, it has not always been possible to identify the sources of all the material used, or to trace all copyright holders. If any omissions are brought to our notice, we will be happy to include the appropriate acknowledgements on reprinting and in the next update to the digital edition, as applicable.

Key: Int = Introduction.

Photography

The following photographs are sourced from Getty Images.
Int: Hero Images; SDI Productions/E+; Snapshots from *Own It Projecct Book 2* pp. 26–29, 59,71; MachineHeadz/iStock/Getty Images Plus; code6d/E+; ilyast/DigitalVision Vectors; Snapshot from *Own It Student's Book 2* p. 30; FatCamera/E+; RobinOlimb/DigitalVision Vectors; Visual Generation/iStock/Getty Images Plus; Wavebreakmedia/iStock/Getty Images Plus; Bombaert/iStock/Getty Images Plus; Snapshots from *Own It TRB2* Culture pages from Units 1 & 7.

Typesetting: TXT Servicios editoriales

Cover design and illustration: Collaborate Agency.

Editing: Andrew Reid